From Traum... To JOY

Even in the Midst of Suffering

The

Ignatian

Way

Thora Wease

St. Iggy's Girl Press LLC

East Lansing, MI

St. Iggy's Girl Press LLC

Published via

CreateSpace/Amazon.com

ISBN – 13: 978-1974556403

ISBN – 10: 1974556409

Copyright © 2017

All Rights Reserved

Printed in the United States of America

In Gratitude

To God the Father,

Who created everything in the universe.

To Jesus the Son,

Who became my Companion

in my darkest hours.

To the Holy Spirit,

Who healed me and taught me

how to forgive and love again.

To the Ordinary People

Who said "Yes" to becoming Jesus'

hands and feet on earth, helping me recover,

every day, in so many ways.

To the Professionals

Who used their education and skill,

to help heal my mind, body and spirit.

To the Anonymous Folks

Who prayed for me, so the power

of Angels and Saints did battle for me.

A.M.D.G.

Dedicated

To Joshua Matthew & Christian Catherine,

May God Bless and keep them, always.

Table of Contents

Chapter Four

26

Chapter Five

39

Characteristic #2

Gives ample scope to imagination and emotion as well as intellect

Chapter Six

57

Characteristic #3

Seeks to find the divine in all things—in all peoples and cultures, in all areas of study and learning, in every human experience, and (for the Christian) especially in the person of Jesus.

Chapter Seven

71

Characteristic #4

Cultivates critical awareness of personal and social evil, but points to God's love as more powerful than any evil.

Chapter Eight

90

Characteristic #5

Stresses freedom, need for discernment and responsible action.

Chapter Nine

121

Characteristic #6

It empowers people to become leaders in service, men and women for others, whole persons of solidarity, building a more just and humane world.

Chapter Ten

115

Additional Resources

120

Read This Anyway

Non-fiction books often start with an introduction—one that most people skip. This is a book about healing and finding joy so if you're reading this, I'll bet you're impatient for the healing to begin. Great. Let's start here and get right to it. This book is about three things: (1) Exploring Ignatian Spirituality; (2) how Ignatian Spirituality helped me recover from life-altering traumas, and (3) how it can help others, to heal their wounded spirit and find true joy, even in the midst of suffering.

While P.T.S.D., O.C.D. and other symptoms that often accompany Life-Altering Traumas are discussed, it is only in the context of my own personal experience. This book, in no way, claims to be an authoritative treatise on *psychological* treatment. It is first and foremost, about Ignatian Spirituality and my personal journey to heal the *spiritual wounds* left by my own traumatic events. Although the book was born out of the dire need for a book that incorporates the Faith and traditions of a Catholic Christian in the healing process (there was none), *From Trauma to Joy* is accessible to anyone and everyone who has suffered a life-altering trauma. I am a theologian and writer by education, a Catholic by choice, and a trauma survivor. Those are my credentials—along with decades of psychological "treatment," individual research and spiritual direction. I have endeavored to avoid dense theological and psychological language and to speak to you as one broken heart to another. We will progress through the Six Characteristics of Ignatian Spirituality, utilize the great wealth of help available and do all we can to help ourselves (it's much more than you think).

Having said that, this is not your typical "self-help" book. Primarily, because the first thing I am going to tell you is that you *cannot ever heal your "self" by yourself.* The reason is that you are thrice broken. The human person consists of mind, body *and* spirit, the three are intertwined and interdependent and therefore so is our woundedness.

Darrell Scott, clearly a man in Post-Traumatic Event Recovery, addressed the House Judiciary Committee's subcommittee after his daughter, Rachel, was one of the victims of the Columbine High School Shooting:

> *"Men and women are three-part beings. We all consist of body, mind and spirit. When we refuse to acknowledge a third part of our make-up, we create a void that allows evil, prejudice and hatred to rush in and wreak havoc."*

A trauma big enough to be life-altering will, undoubtedly, affect *all three* areas, to varying degrees but, *all three* must receive treatment. The problem with some healing methodologies is that, until the fairly recent resurgence of holistic medicine in the West, treatment was separate, compartmentalized, rather than whole. The medical doctors took care of the body, the psychiatric community addressed the mind and if the person had a faith, perhaps their pastor gave them some guidance here and there. Each profession acted independently and sometimes at cross purposes, as you will see later.

It is in those "science only" methodologies that post-trauma sufferers are most shortchanged, by having their spiritual wounds ignored and often, as a result, they never seem to "get over it" even after decades of psychotherapy. Sometimes the "science only" therapists dismiss faith and religious practices as unimportant or worse, as I was told by one such therapist: "Faith and religion are needless crutches that make you weak and dependent. They *must* be abandoned or you will never heal." The only thing I abandoned was that therapist.

So, what qualifies as a life-altering trauma? Again, I am not a clinician, so I have settled on this simple, three-part definition of a Life-Altering Trauma:

Life-Altering Trauma: (1) A sudden, violent (as in forcefully shocking) event that could neither be anticipated, prevented, nor terminated-at-will. (2) An event that renders a person vulnerable to, and helpless against, victimization. (3) As a result of the event, the person's quality of life is drastically and forever altered—physically, mentally *and* spiritually.

While I employed both conventional medical and psychological treatment over the course of forty years—thirty of which I was misdiagnosed and erroneously treated—in the end, Cognitive Behavioral Therapy was the therapeutic mode successful in addressing my P.T.S.D. But it was the *simultaneous*, spiritual direction that complemented and completed what medical and psychiatric practitioners began. In addition to the medical doctors, psychologists and priests/spiritual directors who helped me heal, there were two other components.

The first, was my own personal commitment to healing. I had to ask myself: "What am I willing to do to heal?" The answer was: *whatever it takes.* That *must* be your answer too. The reason? Healing is messy, at times ugly, often painful, and almost daily, for a while, tearful. Remember the Rocky movies? The grueling hard work, the blood, sweat and tears that were shed for victory? That's what we're facing now. This blunt-talk stops some people before they start, but unlike the trauma-pain you're enduring, this temporary, recovery-pain has a purpose—to heal you, to help you find the joy that is out there waiting for you. Like yanking a dislocated shoulder, in the end, everything will be put back in its rightful place. You will be stronger, healthier.

Remember, I said there were four components: (1) medical & psychological treatment (2) Spiritual Direction (3) personal commitment to healing and the last one is supernatural—Grace. The power of the Holy Spirit, the blood, sweat and tears Jesus shed *for us* on the cross and the grace of God the Father are available to us 24/7, with no copay and pre-existing conditions welcome.

In recovery, we are, indeed, walking "through the valley of the shadow of death" (Ps: 23) and Jesus *is* walking with us every step of the way. While it is true that our healing is directly affected by the effort we put into it—that effort must also include cooperating with the Holy Spirit—and that isn't always easy. However, an encouraging fact is that once we ask God to be our Great Physician—He will never quit, He will never give up on us, until He has completed the work in us that He has begun. It's a promise and He keeps his promises.

"I am confident of this, that the one who began a good work among you will bring it to completion by the day of Jesus Christ." (Phil 1:6)

Since we are adopting what St. Ignatius calls his "Way of Progressing"—toward a deeper, lifelong relationship with Jesus who said: "I am the Way, the truth and the light" (John 16:4), let us refer to *our* deliberate actions and choices toward healing as *Making our Way*. Self-help implies going it alone. *Making our way* leaves room for Jesus to walk beside us, for the intercession of the Angels and Saints and for our professional healers along with other mortal companions to join us in this journey. Trauma notwithstanding, aren't we *all* just trying to *make our way* in this world? What really matters is which way we are going. Let us move toward the One who can heal us.

Healing the spirit is often referred to as Spiritual Warfare because:

"For our struggle is not against enemies of blood and flesh, but against the rulers, against the authorities, against the cosmic powers of this present darkness, against the spiritual forces of evil in heavenly places,"   *(Ephesian 6:12),*

and never more so than after a life-altering trauma. Why? Because trauma shakes us to our very soul—and our soul is the prize that the enemy wants to capture.

Since it is *Spiritual Warfare,* please indulge my use of military terminology. First, let me introduce the troops: God the Father, Jesus the Son and the Holy Spirit will be our High Commanders. Next, who better than our warrior saint, St. Ignatius, to be our General? For now, I will be your Platoon Sergeant. All the Angels and Saints in heaven, the doctors, therapists, spiritual directors, and finally, a few precious friends and relatives here on earth, will become your band of brothers. See, you are not alone. I will repeat that: You are not alone. Say it aloud: "I am not alone." Good.

I know, your traumatic event has left you drained, raw and tired-to-the-bone from dealing with all the changes in this *different you* and your equally strange and altered life. Experiencing these changes among loved ones who have no more clue than you do, about what's going on or, what to do *for you*, is both frustrating and discouraging—for everyone. How could they understand? You don't fully understand it yourself. The very *last thing* you want right now is to be drafted into a war that you didn't start. I know, I remember lying in bed and angrily crying out: "No more—wasn't the trauma itself enough suffering?" This new challenge is not more suffering born of another person's sinful act or their evil choices, but so much more—this is a chance to put order back into a life that has been violently dis-ordered; this is a chance to see and experience God's Grace up-close and personal, this is a chance to turn victim into victory. Think back to "Rocky" and keep your eye on the prize: For us, it is peace and Joy.

I recently found an anonymous author's response to a reader's challenge that the author's memoir was too blunt. The author responded: "I can be of more help to you in my brokenness than I ever could in my pretended health." I will attempt to be that honest.

Because this is not a memoir, per se, some graphic descriptions from my traumas remain where they belong: in a blue cloud hanging over my therapist's couch, at the foot of the Cross, or in the confessional, for two reasons. First, this book, even though I use my life and recovery as examples [I have no right to use anyone else's], *isn't about me at all*; our focus needs to be inward toward "cleaning our own corner" and then upward whence comes our help.

First, let's take a couple surveys just so *you* can see where you are. Please use a pen or highlighter to indicate *all* that apply to you (or your loved one). Checking these boxes does not mean that you have P.T.S.D., only a qualified therapist can determine that, but if you checked even one of these events, and you still use the self-defense mechanisms in Survey #2, or frequently experience the emotions listed, in relation to your event, then *something is disordered* in your life and bears further exploration.

After you've finished those, we'll move on to a fascinating glimpse of St. Ignatius and the history of the Society of Jesus (Jesuits), and how Ignatian Spirituality came into being and, more importantly, how it can help us *make our way*.

Life-Altering Trauma

Survey #1—Event

Please Check or Highlight all that Apply to You.

Abortion	Botched	Against Will	Minor Child	Voluntary
Accidents [Horrific]	Auto/Bus	Trains/Subway	Planes/Falling	Boats
Act of Nature [Earth]	Earthquake	Volcanos	Sinkhole	Floods
Act of Nature [Weather]	Hurricanes	Tornadoes	Blizzard	Tsunamis
Animal Attack	Dog	Bear [wilderness]	Other Animals	Shark
Assault [body]	Bully	Knife/Gun/Weapon	Attempted Murder	Mugging
Buildings /Structure	Arson	Building Collapse	Bridge Collapse	Elevator
Captivity	Domestic	Human Trafficking	P.O.W.	Kidnapping
Childhood Abuse	Physical	Psychological	Sexual	
Chronic Disease	Debilitating	Disfiguring	Chronic Pain	Terminal
Death of A Loved One	Witness to	Murdered	Suicide	
Domestic Violence	Stalker	Bodily Assault	Mental Abuse	
Explosions	Bomb U.S.	Bomb Foreign Soil	Gas Lines/Arson	
First Responder	Accident	Terrorist Attack	Suicide	Grisly event
Near Death	Illness/Accident	Suffocation	Violence	Drowning
Neighborhood Violence	Drive By	Robbery/Gunpoint	School Shootings	Gangs
Sexual Assault	Date Rape	Stranger Rape	Pedophile	Incest
Witness-Extreme Violence	Murder	Violence against Family/ Loved One	Genocide	Gore of War
Other:				

Great job! There is no "good" score; there are no right or wrong answers. Like I said, this is not a diagnosis of P.T.S.D but, even a single checked box indicates there might be spiritual wounds that need to be healed. After a few words about P.T.S.D. we'll check out Survey #2.

A Few Words about P.T.S.D.

The P.T.S.D.gov website estimates: "7.8% of American's will experience P.T.S.D. at some point in their lives with women twice as likely as men to develop it. About 3.6 percent of adults aged 18-54—that's 5.2 million people—have P.T.S.D. during the course of any given year." That's five million people suffering, right now. So even if you don't have P.T.S.D., if you're suffering, you *are not alone.*

Another important distinction that is often not made by the psychiatric community is that Post-Traumatic Stress Disorder is not a personality disorder like narcissism or caused by a chemical imbalance in the brain like Bi-polar disorder.

Post-Traumatic Stress is a BODY/SENSE-MEMORY of a traumatic event of such magnitude that it becomes coded on the cellular level. This has been proven by viewing the brain scans of people with P.T.S.D. while they are shown images that "trigger" a symptomatic response. The brain, the cells, have recorded, imprinted, if you will, the information that this "trigger" signifies danger and initiates the adrenaline fueled fight-or-flight response.

Because our defense mechanisms against a "perceived threat" [that only we experience] may make us behave in a way that the world generally considers "crazy" or we may respond in a variety of irrational, distant or uncommunicative habits, the treatment of P.T.S.D. has fallen under the care of mental health professionals. A person with P.T.S.D. may have other issues that are, indeed, within a category of a personality disorder or mental illness—**but P.T.S.D. itself, is not a mental illness**—despite its inclusion in the psychiatric diagnostic bible: the DSM-V.

There are many excellent P.T.S.D. workbooks as companions to therapy and also new and exciting Virtual Therapies available for Soldiers and First Responders and those who have P.T.S.D. as a result of war and natural disasters. Again, I am not a clinician and each person must seek out and find the treatment option that is best for them. The Veteran's Association and various projects offer a wide range of opportunities for healing, from bonding with wolves to virtual reality desensitization. Here, we are dealing with the spiritual wounds and while I refer to my own CP.T.S.D. recovery using Cognitive Behavioral Therapy, I do not infer that it is the best therapy, only that is was best for me, and I use it as a demonstrable example of integration of body, mind and spiritual treatments.

Every journey begins with a point of origin and for us, the point of origin is our own traumatic event. While not everyone who has a traumatic event will end up with Post Traumatic Stress Disorder [P.T.S.D.] or exhibit the symptoms associated with it, we need to make sure that, for clarity we all *start* at the same place. One of the key factors in determining Post Traumatic Stress Disorder is *the duration of difficulty recovering* from the traumatic event. Many traumas are one-time events, that while, traumatic at the time, once physical healing has taken place the residual mental and spiritual damage are minimal by comparison and short-term. The time-frame for determining P.T.S.D. is generally, debilitating post-trauma symptoms that last longer than three months. Operative word: debilitating.

For example, if someone's loved one dies unexpectedly they may, after time and/or grief therapy, come to terms with it even though, the rest of their life will, of course, truly, never be the same. This is not meant to minimize one person's pain compared to another. Anyone who suffers can find comfort within these pages. However, say, the person had a fight with the deceased right before the person committed suicide and they were the person who also found the gory mess—the shock and guilt may be of such depth and duration that a diagnosis of P.T.S.D. could be made. It is *always* a case by case basis—every human psyche and soul are unique, no matter how the clinical world wants, and relentlessly tries, to put us in nicely labeled boxes. You are unique.

Since the variety, intensity and repeated nature of traumas I experienced left me with a form of P.T.S.D. called *Complex* P.T.S.D. I'm going to differentiate between the two. These definitions are from the National Center for P.T.S.D. on the Veteran's Administration Government website [see links in Resource section].

Basic Post Traumatic Stress Disorder

*Lasts longer than three months

*Causes great distress, anxiety

*Disrupts work or home life

*Reliving the event: May also include nightmares, flashbacks, susceptibility to "triggers" you may see, hear or smell that causes you to relive the event.

*Avoiding situations that remind you of the event

*Negative Changes in your beliefs and feelings—you may avoid relationships

*You may forget about parts of the actual trauma <u>or</u> not be able to either stop thinking about it; or you may not be able to speak of it at all.

* Feeling keyed up, hard time sleeping, always on the lookout for danger, trouble concentrating, easily startled and the startle reflex is exaggerated, desire to have back to a wall for clearer view of potential dangers.

Complex P.T.S.D.

In addition to all of the above—for the P.T.S.D. to be "Complex" the traumatic event itself was long-term, ongoing, and the victim is held in some form of captivity either physically or emotionally. "In these situations the victim is under the control of the perpetrator and unable to get away from danger."

Consciousness. "Includes forgetting traumatic events, feels detached from one's mental processes or body."

---

*Self-Perception. "May include helplessness, shame, guilt, stigma, and a sense of being completely different from other human beings."

*Distorted Perceptions of the Perpetrator. "Attributing total power to the perpetrator, becoming preoccupied with the relationship to the perpetrator, or preoccupied with revenge."

*Other Issues with chronic trauma include: Using alcohol or other substances to avoid and numb feelings related to the trauma, self-mutilation or other forms of self-harm.

While the treatment for both P.T.S.D. and CP.T.S.D. is essentially the same, survivors with <u>C</u>P.T.S.D., need *extra help* restoring their control and power. This is done by establishing healing relationships that create *safety, allow for remembrance and mourning and promote reconnection with everyday life.*

And now that you have identified the life-altering traumas you have experienced [or a loved one], please take the survey on the next page and mark any symptoms or feelings that are still present affecting your life and health.

Survey #2 – Residual Effects of Trauma

Please Check or Highlight all that Apply to You

Issues	General	Specific	Severe
Avoidance	Crowds, Events, Church, Formerly enjoyed events	Friends, Family Relationships	Live as a Recluse, Agoraphobia
Mental Difficulties	Difficulty Concentrating, Short-term memory loss	Insomnia, flashbacks, nightmares	Memory loss around event/ period of life
Depression	Lethargy, Lack of Interest in usual activities	Loss or gain of weight, sleeping too much	Suicidal Ideations
Employment Problems	Trouble keeping jobs, change jobs often	Lose jobs due to absenteeism	Lose jobs due to violent "incidents"
Fearful Responses	Hypervigilant [always on lookout for danger]	Easily Startled, Panic Attacks, flight response	Paranoid, Violent responses
Self-Harm	Risky Behaviors not in best self-interest	Promiscuity, self-medicating with alcohol or illicit drugs	Self-mutilation, Suicidal Thoughts or Attempts
Disorders	Obsessive Compulsive cleaning/repetitive actions	Eating Disorders	Personality
OTHER			

Feelings and Emotions STILL Frequently Experienced

Anger (Generalized)	Fear (Paralyzing)	Out of Control (Scare Myself)	Guilt (Overwhelming)
Rage (Revenge Quality)	Abandoned By God	Sadness (Unending)	Feel Unlovable
Helplessness	Victimization	Despair	Self-Loathing

Great job. There is no score. There are no right or wrong answers. This was just *for you*, to get an idea of things that might be dis-orderd in your life. To help us with that, let me introduce you to our Warrior Saint and our Band of Jesuit Brothers.

Chapter One

Lifestyle of the Jesuit and Fameless

St. Ignatius of Loyola (1491-1556) born San Ignacio de Loyola, baptized Iñigo, was the youngest son of a noble and wealthy family in Spain. He became a soldier, a courtier and was quite the ladies' man. He was bold, vain and sensual with a great ambition to win renown. He enjoyed romantic tales of knights and their exploits and delighted in music—especially sacred hymns. Ignatius stood a mere five foot two with an abundance of reddish hair.

In 1521, at the Battle of Pamplona, Ignatius was wounded. One leg and knee badly fractured and the other wounded as well. To complicate matters, the original treatment had set the bones incorrectly and so he endured several excruciatingly painful re-breaks and surgeries. Ignatius was left with a limp. During his recuperation, he did not have access to the romantic tales he preferred, but only to the lives of the Saints. Ignatius experienced a gradual spiritual awakening when he came to realize that his contemplations of worldly things left him empty and unsatisfied while the lives of the Saints were inspiring and fulfilling.

Not to minimize all that Ignatius was into a few short paragraphs, but the product of his life, into which we will immerse ourselves, will give a more faithful rendering. He believed that deeds speak loudest. After recovering from the Battle of Pamplona, Ignatius left his family, made a holy pilgrimage and spent *three full days* confessing the sins of his entire life. He hung up his sword near the statue of the Virgin Mary as a symbolic "giving up" of his worldly ambitions. He then spent nine months living as a beggar and underwent a severe lifestyle neither bathing nor trimming his hair or nails. While he gained a sense of an interior light and joy during that time he also came to understand that such severity was not what God wanted from him—that attention to his interior life was most important.

Ignatius embarked on more pilgrimages that included one to Jerusalem where he wanted to remain, but his vision for a new order was misunderstood by the priests already there, so he returned to Spain and then on to France for a period of study. There, he made friends who would become the first members of the Society of Jesus. Ordained in 1535, before the completion of his theological studies, Ignatius left Paris due to ill health. Now, age forty-nine, he and his companions went to Rome. On September 27, 1540 Pope Paul III gave permission for the founding of the Society of Jesus. We know them today as the Jesuits. Ignatius was, not surprisingly, elected the first General of the Society.

As General of a new band of warriors—*spiritual* warriors, Ignatius set about writing *The Constitutions* and the *Spiritual Exercises* that were the foundational rules and training manual for the novices joining the order. Ignatius called it the "Way of Progressing." These instructions and writings are what we will use to help us *make our way* and if you are like me, they may, at first, be a roadmap on the journey to healing but eventually, to a lifelong adoption of the "Way of Progressing" that is known as Ignatian Spirituality.

There are several things that stand out in Ignatian Spirituality. One of the first things is the Jesuit vow to never *seek* fame, higher office or the Papacy. Priests, Bishops and Cardinals are first, mortal men and so, like everyone else, have a capacity for excessive ambition and greed as well as a great capacity for holiness; the vow to not *seek* fame helps keep temptation away. While we now have our first Jesuit Pope, Pope Francis, he neither sought the office, nor was he climbing the ladder to success or politicking—but rather quietly living out the "Way of Progressing" in Argentina.

That is not to say that Jesuits live an anonymous life in prayer. While they do not *seek fame* many Jesuits have become well-known because of their accomplishments as the founder of hundreds of schools and universities in eighty countries, also as the most fervent missionaries in history, evangelizing across the globe. Jesuit explorers founded the city of Sao Paulo, charted the Amazon and Mississippi rivers, brought rhubarb, quinine, vanilla and ginseng back from Asia and South America and are believed to have introduced the umbrella to the West. Jesuit Anthanasius Kirchner was the first to discover that the Bubonic plague was spread by microorganisms, and Jesuit mathematician, Christopher Clavius, created the modern Gregorian calendar.

You can pursue your gifts, talents and passions and *still* answer the call to holiness.

They are scholars, authors, editors, publishers, doctors and scientists. Even possibly the least known achievement is a 17th century Jesuit drama teacher who invented the trap door. What this proves, beyond any doubt is that you can pursue your gifts, talents and passions and *still* answer the call to holiness. And since each of us only get twenty-four hours in a day, the Jesuits have proven that Ignatian Spirituality is realistically "doable" regardless of our demanding careers and lives.

One way Jesuits keep their promise to eschew self-aggrandizement is being ever mindful of a term you may have seen: A. M. D. G., short for *Ad Majorem Dei Gloriam. This is the unofficial motto of the Jesuits: *For the greater glory of God. What that means is that whenever there is a choice to be made—regarding anything—they vow to make whichever choice gives the greater glory to God. It also means that any work, as long as it is not evil, can be considered giving glory to God. While one's accomplishments may certainly be recognized, and praise accepted with humility, one should make sure that the *greater glory* is always given to God.

Gratitude, joy and simplicity are the warp and woof of Ignatian Spirituality, along with a generous dose of laughter. Ignatius said: "Laugh and grow strong." Laughter is especially important while recovering from a Life-Altering Trauma, and in facing the sobering changes brought on by our own personal *Pamplona. It is not too far-fetched to think that perhaps St.

Ignatius was suffering from some of the symptoms of Post-Traumatic Stress Disorder. He certainly understood it well.

Finally, is the daily prayer of St. Ignatius that is prayed and lived by every Jesuit, called the *Suscipe:* Latin for "receive," it is also the first word of the prayer that begins the Latin Mass.

Suscipe

Take, Lord, and receive all my liberty,
my memory, my understanding,
and my entire will,

All I have and call my own.
You have given all to me.
To you, Lord, I return it.

Everything is yours; do with it what you will.
Give me only your love and your grace,
That is enough for me.

Beautiful and yet profound in its simplicity. Just like Ignatian Spirituality, it is straightforward. The ultimate goal is for a Jesuit's entire life is to become a *living prayer* and that their actions become what is called "Contemplation in Action." Ignatius always believed that deeds speak loudest.

Jesuits get to that place of sanctity and joy by frequent self-examination, both Examination of Conscience before making a good confession, and in what they call "The Examen:" a daily (or sometimes thrice daily) check-up of both the great and wondrous interaction of God in their lives as well as, where they may have fallen short of the goal.

A New Battleground

Although Ignatius put up his sword, he spent the rest of his life preparing his Jesuit brothers for life's spiritual battles. We identify a *physical* battle when we say someone is battling cancer. We acknowledge a *mental* battle when someone is battling depression. But seldom do we pay attention to the *spiritual* battles going on around us, much less the battle raging within our own soul. That is the war we must now wage. Recovery from a life-altering trauma is without doubt, Spiritual Warfare. The traumatic event left us battling an emotional roller coaster of fear, anger, sadness, bitterness, and a whole litany of associated life-change issues.

Our first spiritual battle is against the desire for revenge and the confused feelings regarding "Our Father" who, until our traumatic event, we had thought of as our Protector but who, this time, didn't protect us or someone we loved—or so we thought.

But St. Ignatius has laid out our battle plan. He enumerated *Six Characteristics* that are present in a *healthy* Ignatian Spirituality that will help us *make our way* toward the joy that awaits us. We will explore each of these *Characteristics*, including Journaling Assignments and prayers to help change them from ideas into healthy habits incorporated into our lives.

First, we will take a look at all six as a preview of coming attractions:

Six Characteristics of a Person who Embraces Ignatian Spirituality:

1. Sees life and the whole universe as a gift calling forth wonder and gratefulness.

2. Gives ample scope to imagination and emotion as well as intellect.

3. Seeks to find the divine in all things—in all peoples and cultures, in all areas of study and learning, in every human experience, and (for the Christian) especially in the person of Jesus.

4. Cultivates critical awareness of personal and social evil, but points to God's love as more powerful than any evil.

5. Stresses freedom, need for discernment, and responsible action.

6. Empowers people to become leaders in service, men and women for others, whole persons of solidarity, building a more just and humane world.

One of the many beautiful things about Ignatian Spirituality's flexibility is that just as Jesus meets us where we are, hot mess and all, so too, can our Ignatian journey begin where we need it most. Right after a trauma, or in cases (like mine) where none of the perpetrators were ever punished, where there was no "justice" via our legal system nor was there emotional closure before they died, it was easy to get stuck on the evil done *to me*, rather than God's love *for me*. I wanted nothing to do with any Characteristic that talked about gratitude. To me, that expectation and would happen alongside flying pigs. But as you'll see, St. Ignatius really knew his stuff.

Chapter Two

Characteristic #1

"Sees the whole universe as a gift calling forth wonder and gratefulness."

When I was in my early teens I was removed from my family home for a summer, initiated by the family court system and sent to a distant relative of sorts—a family friend I called "Aunt," who had been a rural, farm missionary and ran a small Bible church out of her garage. She was in her mid-sixties then, had raised more than a dozen children of her own and all but a disabled son, were grown and gone by the time I arrived.

The courts had become aware, via a school counselor, of some inappropriate and abusive behavior on the part of my grandmother who lived with us. I had testified to events as honestly as possible while carefully protecting my most damaging abuser, my mother. Mother was "urged" by the court to *voluntarily* remove me from the home while they sorted things out. My California classmates thought I was just vacationing in Michigan, something our family did every August, but it became the first steps of a much longer journey.

It was at Aunt's house that I first encountered the concept of a "universal gift" and nurturing an attitude of gratitude—decades before I encountered it again as part of Ignatian Spirituality. I was required, right after bedtime prayers, to write down *three* things I was grateful for or at least three *good things* I had noticed during that day. There was only one rule: I could not write *anything* negative. If something bad happened but had a happy ending, I was only allowed to write the happy portion. Aunt called them our own "Good Books" full of proof from our own life, every day that the Love God professes for us in *His* Good Book, is true.

This planted seeds of a habit that I abandoned a couple months later when the courts returned me to my abusive home [thankfully, sans grandmother] but had not, as I'd secretly hoped, uncovered the whole truth—a truth I was too terrified, to indoctrinated to silence, to speak aloud. I abandoned the practice, not because of the horror of being returned home, but because I recognized the *danger* of my mother getting her hands on my thoughts, which were, I thought, the only untouchable thing I had in my life. It turned out that she had invaded those too with masterful brainwashing that would manipulate me for decades. Once out of the house at eighteen, I would resume the practice, sporadically, along with journaling that included more than just gratitude. Thoughts. Dreams. Worldly concerns and even open letters to God.

Journaling

Journaling has been around for millennia and some of the greatest works ever written were the authors (Saints) writing *to themselves* or to God. It is also important for *us* to record this journey for both clarity and later reflection. Since we have already checked the boxes of both

Enemy #1: The Traumatic Event and Enemy #2: The Dis-Ordered coping mechanisms, let us now get out a journal (a spiral notebook will do nicely) and write about **God's love for us and God's gifts to us.**

When I was asked to do this, I screamed inside my head: "If one more person tells me to count my blessings!" It wasn't just that I was plenty angry at the injustice of it all, I had tunnel vision, focused only on what I'd lost and how the all-powerful as in All-Mighty God *could have* stopped it from happening… but didn't. If that's where you are, right now, it's okay. This exercise isn't going to be about *that,* nor is it attempting to discount your pain one iota.

Note to Loved Ones

Do not, ever. I repeat: *ever* say to a wounded soul any sentence that begins with "At least…" "*At least* you didn't die. *At least* you still have *one* eye, hand, or leg. The worst example I ever encountered was to a friend who lost her child. I'm sure you can guess where I'm going: "*At least* you still have other children at home." Oh, yes, he did.

Most life-altering traumas are not the result of negligence or "asking for it" on the part of the wounded, therefore, trying to make it a zero-sum game discounts the pain and loss that they are suffering. Don't know what to say? That's easy: nothing. *Just be present.* Let them say whatever they need to—without criticism, to "tone it down." I had so much anger I thought I would implode and of course, it spilled out. But rather than someone acknowledging it: "You sound very angry" which might have opened a door for communication, I got wagging fingers and a scolding regarding word choices—angry words were not "Christian." So I withdrew. I didn't need judgment heaped on my pain. I isolated myself and isolation is never healthy.

If a response is required, a non-judgmental "neutral" is always best. "You sound like you are in so much pain. I wish I could make it go away for you. You are important to me." Something to indicate you "hear" them and that you wish the best for them and you are there for them. That is a HUGE gift. It may feel like "not much" but trust me, it is.

Even in the beginning of trauma recovery, when we are still raw, we can, with a bit of effort, find things to be at least minimally grateful for. It might take some searching, but keep trying. Living with an "attitude of gratitude" has great medicinal properties, as you will see. It took me several tries. I didn't want to dilute my anger because it *felt like* losing my power. It's not an either/or. Either be angry about *this,* or appreciate *that.* So for now, let's focus on "that."

Journaling Assignment #1

God's first gift to you? Life, followed by a birthday gift: ALL OF CREATION! What in the universe do you really like? Perhaps, start with the animal kingdom. I simply love birds. A child whose life existed in my small bedroom, sequestered, I envied the birds that could fly away. I loved bird coloring books and I'd endeavor to color them accurately from Audubon books. To this day, one of my favorite possessions is a salt/pepper set of chubby bluebirds from my daughter. For some reason, the giant eyes of the exotic Kinkajou always made me laugh with great glee, as did just saying the word Emu, aloud. I also love my current cat, YumYum.

Moving on to geography. *My favorite place* is the white sand beach on Lake Michigan's Northwestern shore. Yes, "I like long walks on the beach" (insert laughter). The only thing I like better than watching sailboats is being on one. *My favorite sound* is waves lapping against the hull. I like the fall best of all seasons. For me it isn't the dying summer—perhaps because I was born in the fall—to me, it feels like a new beginning. Speaking of new beginnings, *my favorite sport* is baseball because: "every inning is a new beginning" with the possibility of a turn-around for the underdog. See what I mean? Write these kinds of things—we'll come back to it later…but for now just write and write and write some more.

You and your life are so much more than the trauma and pain.

Since God created the heaven and earth—these are all things God created *for you* to enjoy—Gifts He has given *you*. So start with the things *you* like. Which do you like better Sunrise or Sunset? For me it is a tie between 2 a.m. when the world is quiet and the stars seem the brightest and birds singing in the just-before-dawn, as if they are beckoning the sun to rise. What makes you laugh? I have a friend who finds TV shows with people falling down hysterical. She is not a mean person but she finds people falling down hilarious, while I am filled with anxiety for the person and their humiliation and don't enjoy it at all. On the other hand, silly animal videos can keep me laughing for hours. Write it down. What types of movies, music or books do you enjoy? Forget everything else going on in your life right now and write until you can't write any more. It's important to write as many as you can think of. What food is "comfort food?" Find categories of your own to add. Favorite flower? Color? Holiday? Clothing? This is the first of many journal exercises you will do. I used both spiral notebooks and typed on the computer. If you are better at typing than writing—that's perfectly fine. Put them in a three ring binder—but still leave a notepad next to the bed for middle of the night inspirations.

Very important: make sure that <u>no one</u> reads them.

At this point, they are *not* for sharing. They are NEVER EVER for family, friends or spouses—who will instinctively want to challenge, discuss and worst case, maybe even judge what you have written. For now, they are between you and God! Eventually, you may wish to share all or part of them with a therapist or Priest/Spiritual Director—*both of whom, are bound to never tell another living soul. Only that kind of safety allows you to be as honest as you need to be, in order to heal.* Be sure and write in a private place without distractions or interruptions and so as to not generate curiosity in loved ones that they would seek out your journal when you are not around. Especially since, sometimes, you might be writing and suddenly burst into tears. Cry it out if you need to, it's healthy. So you need a place where people won't rush in and demand to know why you are crying. Privacy is an absolute must.

If you can lock your journals up, do so. I know, I sound a bit paranoid but the truth of the matter is that when we write and write and write, we often bring to the surface things that were buried in our unconscious, things that *desperately need to come out* to help us heal, but that might shock others. It is only then, with everything in the light of day, bathed in the Light of Christ, that we can heal. So these writings are *vital* to your recovery, but it only works if *you* are *safe* writing whatever comes to mind. Both you and your journals need to be safe.

I speak from experience. A friend let curiosity get the better of her when she was cat sitting. I lived alone so I thought next to my bed was sufficiently safe. A week or so later she came down on me with that forty-pound Bible of judgment, in a well-prepared tirade, grilling me as to whether I had *truly repented* from the abortion I had as young teen. I had written about my anger against my parents for being forced into it rather than being allowed to put the baby up for adoption. I had written, in great detail, for the first time, how I remembered being strapped down while I kicked and screamed and later waking during the procedure (years before Roe vs Wade) and the horrible thing the nurse said about not putting me back "under" so "Maybe she'll think twice." I can still hear the disgust in *her voice* [The irony, of course, being that she was, at that moment, literally, instrumental in helping *kill* my child]. I had poured my whole heart out on those pages. All the pain, the agony, the horrifying memories and the self-loathing that had been trapped for years. It *was* profoundly cathartic. *Until my friend read it.*

With a summary judgment, she pronounced that all the sufferings I had in the past and all that would *surely come* were God's just wrath and punishment and certainly, nothing more than I deserved. There was such self-righteousness in her eyes, her voice dripped with condemnation. It further broke my already-broken heart. I cried for days. Our friendship ended. I had one more person I would have to forgive. Don't let my pain be in vain—take heed, please.

You've now finished two surveys and Journaling Exercise #1. After the next exercise we will move on to Characteristic #2. This one may seem daunting but it's like the joke: "How do you eat an elephant?" Answer: "One bite at a time." We are going to complete our foundation of "Good" with a survey of our entire life. Yes, a whole life, but just *the good stuff.*

But before we do, I want to add something that is important—more important if you are writing about difficult topics in your journal, but something you should always do, since you never know what might come up. Praying before you journal. This is my favorite.

Prayer before Journaling

O. Lord, as I write these words,

Please bring to my mind those events and hurts that

Need to be healed. Help me, Holy Spirit, to remember only what is important.

Help me to be completely honest, even though I am afraid, ashamed.

Help me, O Lord, to cooperate with the Holy Spirit and those

You have generously sent to help me heal.

In Jesus' name, I pray. Amen

Or pray the "Our Father" and afterward, a favorite addendum from "Yielding, Prayers for Those in Need of Hope:"

"God, my Friend, who could count the number of times I've said the "Our Father," how many times I've so incautiously said 'Thy will be done'? Help me say it now and mean it: not my will, Thy will be done. Amen." (Fr. William J. O'Malley S.J.)

Journaling Assignment #2

Taking **five to ten year chunks at a time:**
Write down the very *best memories of your entire life.*
That's right, *your entire life.* Be specific, but since it's just for you, so you can also abbreviate. Write down as many **wonderful memories** that you can, from your *entire* life. Do that now.

  After I moved out on my own, I kept journals sporadically, but kept the bedtime "Good Books" more faithfully and at one point I had seventeen years' worth of them before they got lost during a move. I sometimes wonder what the person thought, who may have found them. I pray that the person saw the great abundance of God's love. I don't have those books anymore, but that doesn't matter because, having done it, *I know without a doubt* that God was with me, blessing me during all seventeen of those, often, difficult years.

  For a moment, let's indulge the last remnant of my O.C.D. [Obsessive Compulsive Disorder] that manifests itself in an affection for numbers and things that add-up. (Insert grins and giggles) If you write 3 good things per day, each year will have 1095 good things to be grateful for. No matter how difficult my life, I could grab any year and have over 1,000 proofs that there was good in my life, and good people in the universe and at the end of those seventeen years it totaled 18,615. Now that's "good" math!

  Everyone's mind tends to remember the bad, the powerfully painful, the emotional damage, but there is an abundance of good all around us. Each year, I quietly take an afternoon right before my birthday and scour the bookstores for just the right journal for the upcoming year. Then I take myself out to lunch! I now include both journal writings and my three "good things" in that one journal. It's something I do for me, only for me, and my soul. This year, my dear friend, Stacey, sent me a journal for my birthday. Some years, I do a separate, smaller, Lenten Journal focused on answering the *call to holiness*, or based on my pre-Lenten Examen— we'll talk about that later. Please, prayerfully consider adopting this habit, forever.

Speaking of Good Books…Let's talk *The* Good Book

Scripture is a great healer and educator. It is important to spend time in the Bible, nourishing ourselves with the Word of God. Maybe you do that already. Maybe you have favorite verses. There are many healing and fortifying *verses* but, if you are still angry or confused about the "God Stuff" in relation to your trauma, you are not going to be receptive to being bombarded by Scripture. But, there are some Scriptures *you desperately need now* and some that are integral to Ignatian Spirituality and designed to help you develop a more intimate relationship with God as you heal. Those I will share…repeatedly.

The following Scripture seems like it was written with the Jesuits in mind; their attitude of gratitude, their constant prayer and their **great joy**. That's what *rejoicing* is: It is to feel, to express, joy. Happiness is contingent on circumstances and fleeting. True joy remains *regardless* of circumstances. I like to think that this is the Scripture St. Ignatius had in mind when he formed the Society of Jesus. I have chosen it as the foundational Scripture for this book.

> *"Rejoice always, pray without ceasing,*
>
> *Give thanks in all circumstances; for*
>
> *This is the will of God in Christ Jesus for you."*
>
> *I Thessalonians 5: 16-18*

Now that you've finished chronicling your worst (the surveys) and best experiences and memories, Journaling Assignments #1 & 2, we are going to *make our way* toward melding the two into a life that cherishes the ups, while weathering the downs.

There will also be a generous sprinkling of prayers throughout the book and I hope you will keep a highlighter handy to mark the ones you find comforting and meaningful. I also encourage you to find a box, or tin and start collecting meaningful "sayings," prayers, prayer cards and inspirational quotes. During some of the roughest months in therapy, my house was plastered with them at every turn—so that as I opened the cupboard, or looked in the mirror, or sat at my desk, there were reminders of God's Love, and notes of encouragement not to give up. Don't forget to include funny memes too!

Chapter Three

Spiritual Warfare 101
Every War has an Enemy—Trauma has Four

The Enemies You Know

The first enemy that will come to mind is the perpetrator or cause/catalyst of the traumatic event—if there was one. The villain with the gun, the rapist, the robber, the drunk who caused the accident, the abusive person in our life. But sometimes the "enemy" isn't so easy to define. It might be an even more indiscriminate villain like a tornado, hurricane or tsunami that victimized hundreds, so you try to write it off as "wrong place, wrong time" and you try to just "get over it" and move on, but you cannot. Every weather report fills you with over-the-top anxiety, you tremble at the sound of thunder or heavy rains. Your house caught on fire because of a frayed wire, you had trouble getting out and now you refuse to own anything that requires electricity. Those are enemies.

The second enemy is a lingering one: The changes in your life since the event. Maybe even, Post-Traumatic Stress Disorder and all the baggage it brings: nightmares, flashbacks, excessive fear, and hypervigilance; the list includes any and all of the symptoms you checked from the opening survey and probably some that weren't listed. Did you skip the two surveys? If you did, please go back and check off all the boxes that apply on both surveys. There is no good score/bad score, this is simply for *your* clarity but it's a vital first step to get the most out of this book. It'll only take a couple minutes. I'll wait.

Those two checklists will help you identify where you may need to pay extra attention or devote more of your time and effort—or it may help you better understand a loved one for whom you are reading this book. Periodically, we will go back and see that some of those symptoms, although perhaps not gone, are more manageable. Around here we celebrate *all* victories.

The Enemies you may not know:

The third Villain that, almost none of the dozens of faith-based books I read *ever* mentioned *directly*, much less told me what to do about him: the devil. He's even so clever he gets himself ranked *third*, if at all, while he is THE GREATEST ENEMY in spiritual warfare. Some people don't believe he exists other than metaphorically. They are wrong. I tell you now:
Yes, there *is* a devil.
Yes, he *is* after you.
Yes, you *are* at war and *your soul* is his prize.

> ## *Pope Francis on the Devil*
>
> "Maybe his (Satan's) greatest achievement in these times has been to make us believe that he does not exist, and that all can be fixed on a purely human level. On this point, there are no nuances. There is a battle and a battle where salvation is at play, eternal salvation; eternal salvation." [Sic]

However, there is an abundance of good news. First, *the* Good News of the Gospels that give us hope and direction, and second, great news regarding the devil's limitations.

Fact#1: The devil cannot physically grab you and drag you into hell against your will.
  (*Hell*, here defined, is total and agonizing separation from God for all eternity).

Fact#2: This means there are only volunteers in hell.
    I repeat.
    There are only volunteers in hell. That's simple. Don't volunteer.

More great news: the devil's arsenal has only one weapon: lies.

*However, the devil's lies are high-caliber, dis-ordered, emotional ammo—and he
    likes to twist Scripture to *back up* those lies.
*He uses the lies you believe about God, about others and about yourself—against you.
*He tells lies that nurture hatred, desire for revenge, grudges, bitterness and violence.
*His lies banish trust, love and mercy and he replaces them with an unforgiving heart.

> *"Our Enemy the devil, who fights with us in order to vanquish us, seeks to disunite us in our houses, and to breed quarrels, dislikes, contests, and rivalries, because while we are fighting with each other, he comes and conquers us, and makes us more securely his own."*
>
> *Saint Philip Neri*

And that leads us to the Fourth, final, and most difficult villain to vanquish—*our own broken and hardened heart*. That's why the emphasis in Ignatian Spirituality is on *knowing yourself in whole and in truth*: your beautiful, worthy, loveable, sinful, weak and broken self. All of it. All of "you" is precious in God's sight.

The Armory

Before we work on any more of St. Ignatius' Characteristics we have to do what any good soldier does before battle: gear up. We have several tasks at hand: Creating a safe encampment in which to recoup-and-regroup after battle. If you live with others, this will be a space apart to pray, reflect and journal. This encampment will be both a tangible space like a bedroom, office, or even garage; somewhere in the real world, as well as, an invisible place, a quiet space within our hearts. After establishing camp and arranging for "private" time, we'll check out the arsenal.

The second protected space we will create is invisible—it is our mind with a direct link to our heart, and it is the most important space. My Aunt used to call it "putting on the Christ Light," as in basking in the Light, Love and Protection of Christ. As I said earlier, the devil *is real* and the closer you get to healing, to challenging and dispelling the devil's lies and to deepening your relationship with Jesus, the *more you will be under attack*, have no doubt.

This *is* Spiritual Warfare and we will begin with a prayer that every Catholic knows: The Prayer to St. Michael the Archangel. My parish says this prayer at the end of every Mass, right before we are sent into the world to "Love and serve the Lord."

For those who may not know, Saint Michael the Archangel is an angel. (The word saint comes from *Sanctus*—Latin for Holy) so Michael certainly is a saint in that regard, but he never lived a human life. He is the leader of all angels and of the army of God. The title "Archangel" means he is above all the others in rank. Only three Archangels are mentioned, by name, in the Bible: St. Gabriel, St. Raphael and St. Michael. St. Michael is mentioned specifically, four times and has four main responsibilities or *offices*, as we know from scripture and Christian tradition.

*The first is to combat Satan.

*The second is to escort the faithful to heaven at their hour of death.

*The third is to be a champion of all Christians, and the Church itself.

*And the fourth, is to call men from life on Earth to their heavenly judgment.

Let us Pray...right now for St. Michael's help.

St. Michael the Archangel,

Defend us in battle.

Be our defense against the wickedness and snares of the devil.

May God rebuke him, we humbly pray,

and do thou, O Prince of the heavenly hosts,

by the power of God,

thrust into hell Satan, and all the evil spirits,

who prowl about the world seeking the ruin of souls. Amen.

Challenge Question: "Wait a minute! My trauma was a real "event" I just need help forgetting it and moving on—why all this devil stuff?"

Answer: Because the devil is standing between you and healing; because the devil wants you broken, bitter and turned away from God. This is *truly* a war of Biblical proportions.

The second task, is to do what we can to protect ourselves. We've met the Troops, our High Commanders of the Father, Son and Holy Spirit; our General, St. Ignatius and now our protector St. Michael the Archangel. It is time to visit the armory where we will collect our vast array of weapons used to wage Spiritual Warfare. It is time to don our spiritual armor.

Putting on Our Armor

"Finally, be strong in the Lord and in the strength of His power. Put on the whole Armor of God, so that you may be able to stand against the wiles of the devil. For our struggle is not against enemies of blood and flesh, but against the rulers, against the authorities, against the cosmic powers of this present darkness, against the spiritual forces of evil in heavenly places. Therefore take up the whole Armor of God, so that you may be able to withstand on that evil day, and having done everything, to stand firm...

Ephesians 6:10- 13

Early in recovery, these are some of the most important words you will speak. Every single day, *before-your-feet-hit-the-floor*, read the paraphrased version on the next page— aloud if you can. Copy the version on the next page, put it on 5x7 cards covered in clear tape for durability, and put one by your bed. I am *completely serious* about wanting you to read it aloud *before* your feet hit the floor. Every. Single. Day. Put another on your bathroom mirror, another in your purse or work desk drawer, and one in your auto glovebox. *Every time* you feel yourself coming under attack (You will learn how to discern that) reread this. This practice also begins our Campaign of Healthy Habits. Read it aloud now and mark the page to remind you to make copies.

Of course, if you are out in public, you need not read it aloud—but first thing in the morning, if you can, do it. It is tremendously empowering and encouraging to hear the words.

The Armor of God

(Ephesians 6:10-13 paraphrased)

Today I put on the helmet of Salvation. Protect my mind from attacks by the enemy, and give me sound thinking.

I put on the breastplate of Righteousness. Guard my heart and emotions from assault. Let me be governed, not by my emotions, but rather by the Truth of Your Word.

I strap on the belt of Truth. Lord, wrap Your Word around me—around the very core of my being. Protect me from error by keeping me in Your Truth.

I step into the sandals of Peace. Use me to take Your peace and Your hope into the world today, and let me stand firm in the face of any attack by the enemy. By anchoring me in Your Word, enable me to keep my footing.

I take up the shield of Faith. Let the attack of the world, the flesh and the devil fall flat against this defensive gear.

Finally, I take up the sword of God: Your Holy Word. Put your Truth in my heart and mind in a fresh way, so that it is able to pierce the hearts and minds of those I encounter.   Amen

Arsenal of Truth

The devil only has one weapon in his arsenal: lies. His lies dis-order, as in mess up or take-out-of-order, our thinking. Our greatest weapon is the truth, both God's Truth and for those of us with P.T.S.D., the truth of our surroundings. Post-Traumatic Stress Disorder is perfectly named if you break it down: the greatest challenge for those of us with P.T.S.D. is that our body and mind are giving us *dis-ordered* information. Health and stability are achieved by breaking down the false messages our brain sends us, to get to the truth. A soldier breaks down his weapon, cleans it and then puts it back *in-order* because, if it isn't reassembled *in-order*, it won't work properly. So too, our brains.

That describes the P.T.S.D. brain: dis-ordered. Some of our *dis-order* is physical: our senses tell us we are *currently* experiencing the pain, the smells, the sounds, even the tastes of that trauma when we are not. Some of our dis-order is in our mind—that's where Cognitive [intellectual activity] Behavioral Therapy can help us retrain our thought processes in discerning and acting on factual input versus faulty "memory." Our Spiritual dis-order is more far-reaching than merely: do we believe in and rely on God? Both mental and spiritual dis-orders begin in the mind, informing our choices and actions.

In computer technology the axiom, GIGO or *garbage in, garbage out*, means that if invalid data is put in, the resulting output will also be invalid. This concept is not a new byproduct of the computer age—it goes back much further. The first time I heard about the importance of what we let into our mind was during the heyday of Self-Improvement books, cassette tapes and gurus. For me, it was Zig Ziglar who used to identify the GIGO mental processes as "Stinkin' Thinkin'" and then went on to instruct the listener how to give themselves a "check-up from the neck up." Around the same time, Steven Covey became popular with his book: "Seven Habits of Highly Effective People" [1989] and a little poem about what thoughts lead to. Most people credit Covey with that quote, but it was also credited to Ralph Waldo Emerson in 1880. I wanted to know the original source. I ended up in 6 B.C. with Lao Tzu, the founder of Taoism. This seems to qualify as, the wisdom of the ages, as valid now, as it was then. It is the strategy we will use in our spiritual warfare.

Watch your thoughts;
They become your words.
Watch your words;
They become our actions.
Watch your actions;
They become your habits.
Watch your habits;
They become your character.
Watch your character;
It becomes your destiny.
Lao Tzu

,

Chapter Four

A *Campaign* of Healthy Habits
Mind, Body and Spirit

In military science, the term *campaign* applies to a large-scale, long-duration strategy incorporating a series of inter-related battles forming a distinct part of a larger conflict often called a war.   And so it is with us—in our Spiritual War we will start with a campaign. We will start the Campaign of Healthy Habits beginning with what we put into our minds always remembering: *garbage in, garbage out.*

Just like breakfast is considered the most important meal of the day, so are our first thoughts. That is the reason behind putting on the Armor of God *before* our feet hit the floor. When I was a single mother of two small children, worked a full-time plus a part-time job while juggling all the responsibilities at home with a 60+ hour work week—and nothing but minimum wage paychecks that needed to stretch further than they ever could—I was always exhausted, discouraged, and overwhelmed by guilt that I only gave my kids short-tempered, tired-time.

Some mornings I would awake with my feet still throbbing from the previous day's sixteen hours of pounding cement floors from table to table, or the muscle strain from bending, lifting and slinging pizzas or raw hands from that housecleaning side-job. To be honest, more often than not, I awoke tearfully disappointed that I did not "die before I wake," because it meant I had to do it all over again and many, many mornings I was certain I couldn't. So I got angry, and anger became the fuel of adrenaline that got me up—sadly, not a mother that either of my kids deserved—and certainly not before school each day.

Back then, I didn't understand the importance of thought-power. My feet hit the floor with dread, resentment and a feeling of failure. It would be twenty plus years before my P.T.S.D. meltdown/recovery would introduce me to a *real practice* of thought power and I could change *Garbage* In/Out to *Goodness* In/*Goodness* Out, regardless of how I feel or what's happening in my life. I now endure chronic pain but even my pain-filled days are greeted differently. The outcome is different too: In spite of the pain, there is peace and there is a joy the pain cannot touch. Yes, **joy** in the midst of suffering!

In a quick recap, we know what trauma befell us and the symptomatic fallout; we've written about what we like about creation, and we've written about our favorite things—and you are, I hope, still writing, every day, those *three things* to be grateful for. These form the foundation for what we are about to expand on with our Campaign of Healthy Habits. So, as Zig used to say, let's give ourselves "a check-up from the neck up!" We're going to start with what messages *about you,* you have taken in, and what you think and say about *you—to yourself*

Our brain is full of "messages" that we have stored from words spoken to us, about us and we have internalized many of them as "true" although they are not. Those stored not-necessarily-truisms form our self-esteem, or lack thereof. Those messages may have come from teachers or other authority figures who "ought to know what they're talking about" or from, more often, our parents or relatives who claim to both know *and* love us best. Just yesterday, a successful television news reporter gave a "shout out" to her 8th grade teacher Mrs. So and So, *"who said I would never amount to anything"* and then looking straight into the camera she said: "look who I'm sitting with"—as she pointed to the President of the United States she was about to interview. That reporter has carried that destructive message *since eighth grade.* It happens. No one is immune.

If you are like me, and come from a house of destructive, hypercritical messages along with physical, emotional and/or sexual abuse, your head is *full* of dis-ordered messages. There's that word again—dis-ordered. And the earlier we got destructive messages, the more out-of-order our view of the world and ourselves became. It becomes what we think when we look in the mirror. It becomes our self-imposed limit of what good things we think we deserve in life.

> "We expect our parents to be perfect but they never are. *No one is.* Part of growing up is learning to forgive them for *simply being human*, and human beings are often wrong. "

I was full of messages from my mother who saw me as her do-over, a chance to relive her happiest days: when she sang and danced on stage at the Fox Theatre in Detroit, as high school cheerleader, college sorority sister, and even her esteemed service in the Navy during WWII. When my foot/leg/hip birth defects prevented coordination to walk correctly, [pigeon-toed, knock-kneed, bowlegged *and* a bit swaybacked] much less the agility required for gymnastics, or the extroversion for cheerleading, or beauty to be prom queen like she was; or lacking the social graces to date the most popular boys, or even my infant-measles-fever-burst eardrum that assured I'd always sing in shrill sharp and off flat, or, or, or—with each failure to live up to her unrealistic expectations she gave me messages about my worth, about my lovability, and even about what I dared, or didn't dare, hope for in the future. The worst was when she would mourn the death of my brother and tell me the wrong child died. Yet, in the same breath, she said "I am your mother and I love you and I only want what is best for you." Can you say mixed message?

Clinically, my mother suffered from Classic Narcissism personality disorder and she was raised by that same abusive mother [grandmother] that the courts insisted she remove from our home if I as to be returned. She chose me, but her guilt was so strong it was almost worse. To top that off, she misused her years working as a child psychologist's researcher [with access to research on manipulating young minds] to experiment on me. Predictably, I became codependent and was quite literally trained in modified POW style. She manipulated food as "reward" [enter my eating issues] and isolation as "punishment" along with psycho-physical abuse. Most notable was her death grip on my shoulder, gouging my clavicle with fingers that typed 100 words per minute on a manual typewriter. She could loft a sixteen pound bowling ball the length of the alley and have it touch down right in front of the head pin. She had a formidable grip. The first time I saw Mr. Spock grip someone like that on Star Trek, I chuckled, wondering if my mother was a Vulcan. Her grip was like a vice—but always where the bruise/break wouldn't show.

I was mostly "captive" in my bedroom. I was allowed to leave for three reasons: meals, chores and convincing neighbors that everything in our house was normal. Bathroom breaks were by permission only [birthplace of bladder issues].

Fortunately, I did not endure the horrendous and now all-too-common scenario of a child kept in filth, chained, locked in the closet or starved—a case where anyone would recognize the abuse in an instant. Hers was calculated and subtle—and held a different kind of hopelessness: that of not being believed. She was personable and articulate and everything "looked" normal. At school I was clean and got good grades. [God help me if I didn't]. Mother frequently pointed out, "who would believe you?" There was no need for a lock on the door, although for a time she painted over my window so I couldn't see other children playing to enhance the solitary confinement effect.

On the one hand, I became her groveling, obsequious sycophant in a sick symbiotic relationship convinced that she and she alone, could see past my vast litany of worthlessness and still love me. [A child never stops wanting their parent to love them. *Never.*] This drastically stunted my emotional development and as predictable, I was an equally deficient mother, as well.

On the other hand, I was her victim just trying to survive by subterfuge—lying and manipulating the way she taught me—counting the days to graduation and escape. The very first thing she taught me was to lie. To keep her lies, to repeat her lies like the script of a complex stage play. If I stuck to the script no one would ever discover what was going on behind closed doors. If I didn't stick to the script there would be pain, there would be retribution. To this day, I cringe when I hear, "what happens in Vegas stays in Vegas" because the household motto was: What happens in this house stays in this house. My reason for sharing all this? To bring home the absolute truth of the next sentence.

We—and our families--are as sick as our secrets.

Because our next exercise is going to be bringing up some tough stuff, perhaps you might want to consider if it is time [if you haven't already] to line up both a therapist and a Spiritual Director. Ignatian Spiritual Directors are trained and certified and you can contact your Diocesan Office for a list of local Spiritual Directors. Your spiritual director doesn't have to be a priest, but certainly someone who is required to keep your secrets, secret. And given our focus on Ignatian Spirituality it might be counterproductive to pick a spiritual director who has no idea what Ignatian Spirituality is.

The last thing you want is for some industrious soul to use you and your misery as a note in a book they are writing. Make sure you tell them—UP FRONT-if they haven't taken a professionally mandated vow of silence, that what you say goes nowhere. Fortunately, following 'the meltdown,' I was blessed to find a therapist who specialized in both P.T.S.D. and women with "mother issues." She was Christian but not Catholic. Luckily my parish priest, at the time, had spiritual direction training. Later, during my years at seminary, I had a single priest who was both confessor and spiritual director because my parish attendance and participation varied based on a parish's CCD and RCIA catechetical needs.

If some of these exercises make you uncomfortable or are disturbing… It IS TIME to get a professional team onboard.

You can easily imagine what kind of garbage was in my head, and what a job it would be to get *all* the garbage out. For that, I have, among those healers listed above, Rev. Robert Schuller, a Protestant televangelist and my friend Bonnie who gave me some of his tapes, to thank. One of his presentations resonated with me on such a meaningful level that I took it to my therapist and we incorporated it into my healing process. I took it one step farther, incorporating another inspirational item from Bonnie and turned it into our next exercise.

Note to Loved Ones

If you want to do something loving—that *really* helps, send gentle, encouraging messages, funny memes, poems, prayers, to them—no big production, just pop them in an envelope with a simple "Thinking of You Today" or cut and paste into an email. I received many messages that amazingly were the *exact one* I needed to hear *that very day.* Help them start their collection now—this is great blessing. Please consider doing it for them regularly.

We will now examine the messages *you* are holding in *your* head—which means, in your wounded heart as well, because our head has a direct line to our heart. Ignatian Spirituality emphasizes knowing and facing the truth about ourselves, our strengths *and* weaknesses, our virtues and our vices—it is only in knowing our *whole true self*, that we can love our whole self. But first, I'd like you to pray this prayer…

Lord, I am in pain, confused and discouraged.

Please reveal the hurtful and bad messages I believe about myself,

Then show me the loving way You see me and want me to see myself.

Help me to reject the garbage and replace it with Your Love.

And Lord, help me to forgive the people who,

Most likely broken themselves,

Gave me the bad messages in the first place. Amen

Journaling Assignment #3: Taking out the Garbage

Take a lined sheet of paper and draw a line vertically down the center dividing it into two halves. This is the "Who I am 'Messages' Grid." It lists what messages you received, from whom, or what you tell yourself. Mine looked like this. Leave the right hand side blank for now. If you can't figure out the message, leave room for later.

Bad Messages:

"You're a worthless, loser" **Step-dad** **Message:** you must always win or you have no worth as a human being.	
"You're never going to amount to anything." **Mom & Step-dad** **Message:** Your future is cast in stone and you cannot change it.	
"I can touch you anywhere I want" **Sexual Abuser** **Message:** Your body is to be used by others, even against your will.	
"You're nobody until somebody loves you" **Mom** **Message:** my worth is based on the social status of having a "man, boyfriend, husband"	

List as many as you can think of. When you have your list, go to the next page and using the "Bell" fill in the right side of the page with WHO GOD SAYS YOU ARE! And, given that God created you, *in His image* [Gen 1:27] **whose Truth do you believe?**

The Bell
I know who I am

I am God's child (John 1:12)

I am Christ's friend (John 15:15)

I am united with the Lord (1 Cor 6:17)

I am bought with a price (1 Cor 6:19-20)

I am a saint   (set apart for God)   Eph 1:1)

I am a personal witness of Christ (1 Cor 12:27)

I am the salt & light of the earth (Matt 5:13-14)

I am a member of the body of Christ (1 Cor 12:27)

I am free forever from condemnation (Rom 8:1-2)

I am a citizen of Heaven. I am significant (Phil 3:20)

I am free from any charges against me (Rom 8:31-34)

I am a minister of reconciliation for God (2 Cor 5:17-21)

I have access to God through the Holy Spirit   (Eph 2:18)

I am seated with Christ in the heavenly realms   (Eph 2:6)

I cannot be separated from the love of God (Rom 8:35-39)

I am establish, anointed, sealed by God   (2 Cor 1:21-22)

I am assured all things work together for good (Rom 8:28)

I have been chosen and appointed to bear fruit (John 15:16)

I may approach God with freedom and confidence (Eph 3:12)

I can do all things through Christ who strengthens me (Phil 4:13)

I am the branch of the true vine, a channel of His life (John 15:1-5)

I am God's temple (1 Cor 3:16); I am complete in Christ (Col 2:10)

I am hidden with Christ in God (Col 3:3); I have been justified (Rom 5:1)

I am God's co-worker (1 Cor 3:9); 2 Cor 6:1). I am God's workmanship (Eph 2:10)

I have been redeemed and forgiven (Con 1:14) I have been adopted as God's child (Eph 1:5)

I belong to God! God Loves ME!

Your Page should now look like the one on the next page. If you can't find the answer in the "Bell," ask your priest or spiritual director, go to your Bible—or pray on it and ask God to show you what to put there.

Journaling Assignment #4: Garbage out   GOOD IN….

"You're a worthless, loser" Step-dad **Message:** you must always win or you have no worth as a human being.	I am assured all things work together for good (Rom 8:28) **NEW** Message: I just have to do my best, win or lose, I am *always* loved by God.
"You're never going to amount to anything." Step-dad **Message:** Your future is cast in stone nobody can change that.	I have been chosen and appointed to bear fruit (John 15:16) I can do all things through Christ who strengthens me (Phil 4:13) **NEW** Message: God has plans for me and God already values me.
"I can touch you anywhere I want" Sexual Abuser **Message:** Your body is to be used by others, even against your will; that is your purpose.	I am God's temple (1 Cor 3:16); I am God's workmanship (Eph 2:10) **NEW** Message: My body is sacred and no one has a right to defile it—not even me.
"You're nobody until somebody loves you" Mom **Message:** my worth is based on the social status of having a "man, boyfriend, husband"	I am God's child (John 1:12) I am a saint (set apart for God) Eph 1:1) I am a citizen of Heaven. I am significant (Phil 3:20) **NEW** Message…I am worthy on my own.

A very wise priest once said to me. "Those parents, teachers etc., they were just people and people are frequently wrong." Now, that's how I l see it. My mother was simply wrong about me. We expect our parents to be perfect but they never are. *No one is.* Part of growing up is learning to forgive them for *simply being human*, and human beings are often wrong.

As you spend more time in your Bible, you will discover additional examples of God's love for you, healthy, loving messages you can use to replace the garbage. So it's Garbage OUT, Goodness IN. Replacing the bad messages with good ones needs to become **a habit.**

The Habit of a Habit

Aristotle described habits as "determinate states of *character* formed by training and giving rise to natural regularities in the individual's actions over time." Again, we see *habit* directly connected to *character.* Longtime habits are literally entrenched at the neural level so change takes time. How much? Theories abound but the general consensus hovers consistently around two months with the disclaimer: individual results *will* vary.

One thing *is* certain: the success of stopping negative habits is enhanced by having something positive to replace them with. Success is also affected by the determination of the individual and their perseverance to hang in there until the desired results are achieved.

Note: it will *always* take longer than you want it to. Be patient with yourself. And, as always, we're back to the question only you can answer? How badly do you want to feel better? Are you willing to give a whole-hearted effort…for as long as it takes?

After finishing the Bell/Grid assignment comes something easy. Besides adding your Bell/Grid to the *Armor of God* that you're already carrying around, you will now prepare your **Emergency Kit.** I had a flat zipper case slightly larger than a 5x7 card. I know a guy who used a roomy pencil case that had holes for a 3-ring binder. We're building a portable First Aid Kit. Chances are you don't have the luxury of not-working while you're working through your "stuff." I didn't, I was in graduate school. But this Kit went with me everywhere.

I experienced several humiliating trigger reactions *during class* but I was blessed to be attending Aquinas College where the professors were understanding and, along with fellow students, immeasurably supportive. I would grab the case [once I was able to move] and head for the hallway or the bathroom and read through my "meditation medicine" until I was calm and my thinking was "in order" again. Even this "action" following a trigger "reaction" was a learned habit. It helped me feel more safe, better prepared, because I had my Kit. Reading the comforting words helped me refocus and quell the embarrassment of having just melted down in public. You already have your *Armor of God*, now add to it both the *Bell* and your completed list with *your NEW messages.*

The reason for carrying the Bell is that once your mind starts challenging bad messages, it will continue and you'll discover more messages that need replacing. Every time you find *yourself* repeating the old messages—yes, our parents and other influential people "programmed us" so well they no longer need be present, because now *we* recite those bad messages to ourselves. We must break that bad habit…and replace it with a positive one. Like Lao Tzu said, everything starts with our thoughts…therefore we must work toward changing our thoughts and habits to create the healthy destiny we want.

Another source of input we seldom think about—while it is *usually* a positive influence in forming our world view and our morals—is the "oral tradition" passed down from ancestors and even our national or ethnic cultures. Until 500 years ago, there was no printing press rapidly mass producing information—good, bad or otherwise, and what we learned was often around the campfire or the dinner table. The adage I remember most vividly is: "If at first you don't succeed, try, try again." I credit my mom's endless repetition of this maxim to my development of dogged perseverance.

My family was, in many ways, typical. I was a child of the 1950's when social scorn was to be avoided at all cost, raised under the guidance of what the nameless group "They" had to say about things. Any sentence that started with the collective opinion of "They say…" was not to be brooked. My mother, although college educated was astoundingly naïve. To her credit, she was also one of the greatest patriots who ever lived. But her patriotism combined with her love of *other people's* wisdom made for some peculiar allegiances. The "they" most often quoted came from my mother's private collection of what she proudly called *Americanisms.* I grew up believing *the source* of her quotes were esteemed *American patriots* because according to Mom, "America is the best, truest nation in the world." That view also accounted for the near-salute when she picked up her weekly National Enquirer and warned me about aliens from outer space, treating the content equal to the Gospels because "American journalists would *never print anything that wasn't true!"* To me, then a preteen, America's 190+ years seemed like plenty of time to give rise to such sage philosophers. Mom's favorite "Americans" turned out to be mostly deceased, non-resident, "immigrants": Buddha, two boys named Tzu: Lao & Sun, Jesus of Nazareth, Confucius, Indira and Mahatma Gandhi, a half dozen rapscallion atheists, scientists and even a foreign warmonger. Who knew Attila the Hun could be so witty? The only *actual* Americans in her repeat-toire, were Eleanor Roosevelt: "No one can make you feel inferior without your permission." And another Roosevelt—Teddy: "Do what you can, where you are, with what you have." We may be what we eat, but we are also chock full of what we *heard* growing up.

Another reason to challenge some of those "messages."

A Few Words about Your Body

We've been focused on mental, emotional and spiritual exercises but they don't burn many calories. When we are stressed—and recovery is a Master Class in stress—our bodies produce cortisol and that tells our body to… well, let's just say cortisol is elevated during times of stress, is connected to adrenaline, cholesterol and is a hormone-based steroid that can cause a whole host of additional problems. And who needs more problems? In increased levels, it can do far worse damage than merely produce abdominal fat that doesn't want to go away. Add to that, the tendency to consume self-medicating "comfort foods" along with a dose of lethargy, often companions of P.T.S.D. and trauma recovery, and you have the recipe for a misery buffet.

Get a Thorough Physical…And Here's Why

I recommend a complete physical as soon as you can arrange it—telling your doctor what's up both physically and emotionally and what you will be confronting in recovery, so *together* you can eliminate medical issues masquerading as emotional ones. How important is this?

Remember when I told you that for thirty years I was repeatedly mis-diagnosed and as a result was erroneously treated? Let me break it down. In my twenties I had reproductive cancer and had to have all my reproductive organs removed—which catapulted me into *early menopause at twenty-six.* Can you say irrational behavior, mood swings and hot flashes? Normal, expected and *not* a mental illness. But my Medical doctor didn't even question a possible *physical cause* my therapist [not even a psychiatrist who is at least a medical doctor] had declared me bi-polar and sent me to be "medicated" with Prozac. Prozac didn't work well with the hormone replacement therapy I was receiving but the two "healthcare providers" *never* talked to each other. Following came my thirties, during which time my thyroid went rogue and tried to kill me—but many of the symptoms were masked by the basket full of rotating psychotropic drugs that my shrink had me on—adding more and more because nothing was "working." Lithium almost destroyed my kidneys, cost me a month in the hospital for kidney flushing and detox and I lost my job.

It took an Iranian refugee psychiatrist [means medical doctor AND psychologist] who was working at the local community mental health until his immigration credentials would let him practice psychiatry in the United States. He said: "You're not mentally ill—you have thyroid disease *and* menopause" and sent me to an endocrinology clinic where I was correctly diagnosed. The third decade? I spent most of it unsuccessfully trying to get the erroneous "bipolar" diagnosis expunged from my records because unlike a medical misdiagnosis—**mental health labels last like tattoos.**

Food for Thought

Also, during your physical, ask your medical practitioner or a nutritionist what foods/diets work best for thriving *amid intensively stressful situations?* And don't stop asking until they take you seriously. Are there vitamins to take, or foods to avoid other than the usual suspects of too much caffeine, alcohol, any illegal drugs and all cigarettes?

I'm now a type II diabetic and my comfort food, of course, is *any* carbohydrate. I have to be extremely careful, and apply more self-discipline that I want to, just to keep my weight steady. But I desire being healthy so fervently that I control my diabetes with food [more like lack thereof—insert laughter] rather than medication. I do need a mega inhaler *with steroids* so I can breathe and move about, which means I also carry about fifty pounds I can't get rid of. Enter low self-esteem because our country is openly cruel to "fat" women and that brings on the shame which, in turn, makes me want to eat a whole bag of potato chips! But this has to be, again, a *conscious choice* to replace bad habits, bag of Oreos versus hummus & celery. No, life isn't fair, but our mental, emotional, and spiritual work requires great energy and brain power so *our food choices do matter.* Remember, we are treating the body and mind as well as, the spirit.

I regularly take a D vitamin because I'm not out in the sun as much as my body needs, I make lots of fresh veggie and fruit plates, healthy stir-fries [low-sodium], and substitute veggie [beans & tofu] protein for most of the meat I used to eat. Part of that is financial, living on disability my food budget is tight; but it is also a great excuse to explore Mexican spices and Asian and Indian vegetarian dishes and flavors! For me, there is an added motivation: I cared for my mom as she died of gangrene poison—a complication from controlling her diabetes with a Krispy Kreme Diet. As I helplessly watched her die a horrendous and agonizing death, I was equally saddened [and enraged] because it "felt like" she didn't care enough about *being around for me or my children* to take care of her health. I remembered that feeling two decades later when I got the diagnosis and a chance to, for once, *truly* be her "do over." So I watch what I eat, faithfully. The upside is there are dozens of fun cooking shows!

We've all heard "Walk the Walk" but let's talk, *The Talking Walk* as in, walking and talking to Jesus. I have limited lung function so I can't "do cardio" without passing out, gasping for air and terrifying those around me. I *can* walk in specific weather conditions, or in large stores… very *slowly.*

I have replaced cardio aerobics with swimming—but again, reduced lung function stops me from reliving my high school "butterfly stroke" days. Instead, I use the foam dumbbells and do my ortho-rehab workout and then tread water in the deep end. I'm up to treading for one hour-forty-five minutes and shamelessly proud of it! Like I said: celebrate *all* victories! Find yours! Do whatever you can—there's always *something.*

Walking keeps the blood flowing, walking keeps our joints limber and walking improves many things. Just being outside is a big help. For those of us with melanoma from our days as sun worshippers or those whose medications prevent direct sunlight exposure—don't forget your vitamin "D." Remember how we're trying to squeeze in all this reflection, thinking and praying time? Try a brief ten-minute walk after dinner or during lunch, while you chat with God, review how your day has been so far. If morning events put me on-the-edge, a lunchtime walk with my Emergency Kit or reapplying my Armor, pull the rest of the day away from the abyss. These little *habits* add up to a great big difference. You will be amazed. The key is consistency.

The last area is sleep. Get enough but not too much. Move and be active enough to get tired, work out, walk, chop wood, whatever gets the blood flowing. It's good to work up a sweat and feel the tiredness in your muscles, if you can. Limit caffeine after mid-day, try sleep-friendly herbal teas in the evening or take a warm bath. If you're having nightmares, see a doctor. I used a short-term sleep aid, for a while, until my therapist and I got the nightmares under control.

Since this is a Catholic book, it goes without saying that frequent [for a year I went daily] attendance at Mass, receipt of the Eucharist and of course, Reconciliation were a HUGE part of my recovery and will be an immeasurable comfort and source of strength for you. It's not as easy as it used to be to enter an empty church any time you might want to—which is sad. A relaxing walk to a church and some silent meditation time is precious and a great blessing. It is what I have always treasured about being Catholic—the Church is available *for us* if not twenty-four hours, at least 365 with daily Mass, when *we* desperately needed it, not just for an hour or two on Sundays and don't forget many parishes have evening hours of adoration—to just sit silently with the Lord.

> **Let's Recap our new Healthy Habits:**
>
> * Putting on our Armor of God, *before* our feet hit the floor.
>
> * Paying attention to diet, meals, and exercise. Seeing a medical practitioner if necessary.
>
> *Remembering to take our Emergency Kit with us--*everywhere.*
>
> * Regularly attending Mass/Eucharist/Reconciliation.
>
> *Staying alert for bad "messages" and consciously changing them to God's Holy Word.
>
> *Taking time to spend some time in silence, to pray [maybe during that walk] and journal
>
> * Doing what needs to be done for a good night's sleep.
>
> * Writing three "good things" about the day before going to sleep at night.

So, how are you doing?

You've been working hard. Pick something from your favorites list and treat yourself. Remember that list of things you liked? Pick one. Pick two. You're *making your way!*

And now, a new daily habit: St. Ignatius calls it "The Examen."

As Catholics, we know the "Examination of Conscience," is recalling our sins before making a good confession. While Ignatius' *Examen* will point to our sins, as always, he emphasizes that we must see ourselves in the "whole truth" which includes the good, the confusing, as well as the weak and sinful. It is a simple, honest, review of the day. What did I do that would have pleased God? What might I have done differently? Were there any blessings today? Did I feel particularly close to God? Was the daily Scripture applicable to today's events? From my Examen, I easily find my three items of gratitude to enter into my nightly journal. I then pray for the areas that need God's grace and help.

It's much like a diabetic checking their blood sugar. Some do it upon rising, some before they eat, some after they eat. *The Examen* is like that, flexible, depending upon what we need and what our real-life schedule is. Ignatian Spirituality is grounded in the real world, acknowledging that we have real-life responsibilities, so the focus is on *simplifying* our everyday life while creating ample time to develop a richer, transcendent, spiritual life.

A Jesuit writer I know does his Examen on the commuter train, another friend chooses to get up an hour before her family so she can do the Examen and *lectio divina* Scripture study. Ignatian Spirituality is full of imagination, as you will see. If I've had an unpleasant encounter with a person [as I did a couple weeks ago] and my response, sadly, was not up to God's standards, my spiritual director [he now lives in my head!] would have suggested I "imagine" that Jesus was there as witness and mediator. What would Jesus have said to the person *in my defense* but...more importantly *for the state of my soul,* what would Jesus have said to me *in her defense?* Knowing that Jesus' speaks only with Love...how would He have suggested this situation be resolved?

As a flawed person, it doesn't always work—because I forget to do it, caught up in the hurt feelings of the moment. Then I need to "take it to the box!" [Confessional]

The Examen in a Nutshell

The daily Examen is a profound technique that helps remove "us" from the emotion of a situation; not just reviewing the cold, hard facts of the day, but using our imagination, we insert Jesus into the events of our day and ask: "What response would have given God greater glory?"

1. Ask for the Holy Spirit's help in recalling all you should.
2. Review all the things you have to be thankful for today.

3. Recall when you felt God's presence the strongest and when couldn't feel God's presence.

4. Ask for guidance in the future and imagine how Jesus' gentle smile with our successes and how compassionate He would be with our failures.

Ignatian Spirituality is grounded in the real world, acknowledging that we have real-life responsibilities, so the focus is on simplifying our everyday life while creating ample time to develop a richer, transcendent spiritual life.

Chapter Five

Characteristic #2
"Gives ample scope to imagination and emotion as well as intellect"

This second Characteristic surprised me. Given the Ignatian emphasis on knowing yourself in full *truthfulness,* it seemed contradictory. Aren't imagination and truth mutually exclusive—the difference between fact and fiction? Not until my undergrad studies in English did I come to realize *why* I am so captivated and moved by some novels. It is because, even though portrayed through fictional characters, fiction often speaks great universal truths with more candid honesty than generally found in society. My own definition regarding the distinction is that *fiction is: the Truth, revealed but with more adjectives.* However, fiction is not to be confused with a lie which is *an untruth told for a self-serving motive.*

It's all about "how you look at it." While, strictly speaking, I was an isolated captive in my house and room, more accurately I was "sequestered" [isolated, hidden away] under an extreme version of "Children should be seen and not heard." Our family's motto was: "Children should be silent always and present *only* for chores or meals." That was my childhood when no one was watching. It was physically dangerous to venture out of my room and be 'noticed.' In the silence of my room I could, without difficulty, hear what was on the television in the adjacent living room of our shabbily built government housing. I listened to stories, to plot lines. Between the quiet "listening" combined with my voracious "reading," it simply followed: I became a writer.

My saving grace was a school librarian who came to "understand" without my having to reveal my circumstances, and who allowed me to bring home all the books my arms could carry—knowing I would have them back early—ready for more. I spent years just "imagining" in my room. It was a six-by-nine foot room with bed, dresser, desk, night stand and built-in closet with barely any space to walk. I had dolls I despised and a few toys in a box I was allowed to bring out on the rare occasions when I was allowed to have friends over—just often enough to keep the authorities at bay, after an observant neighbor "encouraged" Mom to take the beige paint off my bedroom window or he'd need to 'make a call.' No one was more afraid of: "what would the neighbors would think?" than my mother. In that room I learned to *imagine.*

I'd imagine a giant tree on the wall with a rope swing, and birds of all kinds filling the branches and me pumping, pumping my legs until I went so high, I too, grew wings and with the birds, we all flew away. You don't need Freud to figure that one out. There were times when violent and inappropriate things happened and I'd curl up on my bed and cry silently into my pillow, terrified of making any noise because crying was interpreted as "self-pity and ingratitude" and brought further brutality. So I would close my eyes, hug a stuffed animal and *imagine* that I was curled up in the lap of an angel who closed her wings over me like a cocoon—and for years it was only this "image" that would allow me to self-comfort and sleep. Years later, when the P.T.S.D. flashbacks produced some horrific nightmares, I returned to the practice of going to sleep in the lap of *my* angel.

I'd also spend hours imagining families that laughed and did things together. I'd imagine a mother who "loved" her daughter in a less "hands on" and domineering way. I'd imagine doing something—anything— brave and wonderful that would stop my mother from lamenting to God that He "took the wrong child" every time I failed to live up to her expectations. My brother died, on the day of his birth, nearly a decade before I was born—only hours after his father died. Tragically, she lost them both on the same day. Every time, she demanded God explain why He let me live instead of "my precious little Danny" a piece of my heart shattered like crystal on cement. I never understood the either-or-ness of the situation, so I would imagine that my brother had lived and that *he* was my champion, and that he loved me and he was glad that I was alive. I imagined and imagined and imagined. Prisoners instinctively use this technique to stay sane and endure their captivity and isolation.

Of course, imagination can cause problems too. Remember I said "we're as sick as our secrets?" As a child, the only picture allowed on my bedroom walls was the classic Guardian angel watching the little boy and girl cross the rickety bridge while raging waters churned below. Until I was in recovery and had both a therapist and a Spiritual Director—who happened to also be my priest/confessor, I had a secret. Through my journaling it surfaced that I always felt guilty whenever the therapist mentioned my dead brother. At first, I thought it was something like survivor guilt. But after asking God to show me what was going on, since I seemed stuck on that image, I recalled, while journaling, an incident with my mother reciting the litany of how all my failures to please her made her wish, even more, that Danny had lived *instead.* I ran to my room crying and when my eye caught the picture of the children and angel on the bridge…I imagined the children were Danny and me; I imagined pushing him into the water and he floated down the angry river screaming for help; I was glad, remorseless. I just wanted him gone, gone, gone! Then came the crushing guilt and shame. Of course, what I really wanted was for my Mother to stop wishing aloud I was dead. Once I knew that, in reconciliation, I could take the power from the "curse," eventually forgive her—and cut a broken hearted little girl some slack.

So when I encountered encouragement to *imagine* in Ignatian Spirituality I was relieved and overjoyed. I'd worried that so much emphasis on *finding the truth* and re-ordering my mind would find my imaginings in some way wrong. I still spend much time imagining, mostly for writing projects but also for spiritual growth. We are encouraged to imagine how Jesus would defend *us* in a confrontation, and how he would defend *the other person*—in essence: imagine what Jesus would say and do. Imagine Him *with* you. Feel free to imagine Jesus daily.

It is when the Gospels become real to us, that we internalize them and that brings Jesus into our hearts and that will inform our actions, which will become heavenly habits.

Ignatius calls us to imagine ourselves *inside the Gospel stories* as witnesses, walking alongside Jesus, seeing what he sees and in doing so it makes scripture study more *real*. It is when the Gospels become real to us, that we internalize them and that brings Jesus into our hearts and that will inform our actions, which will become heavenly habits. Fr. James Martin S.J., one of my favorite Jesuit authors, has written a book that is perfect for such travels with Jesus. It's called "Jesus, a Pilgrimage" and it's a wonderful threefold adventure. Fr. Martin explains the Biblical history and landscape of the Holy Land during Jesus' ministry; cites the relevant Gospel readings and like a modern travelogue, gives vivid descriptions of the area today. It is perfect for inserting yourself into the Gospels and walking with Jesus.

I was finally able to break the unhealthy habit, of many single people: gobbling my dinner [a bowl of cereal or Ramen] while standing at the kitchen sink, by *imagining Jesus as my dinner guest*. I would imagine a leisurely conversation with him over dinner. My digestive tract appreciated the effort. Where do you need to invite Jesus to join you? Imagine it now. Driving? Chores you don't like? Lonely nights?

When we feel unloved or overpowered by bad messages, we are encouraged to re-read the Bell, for a quick pick-me-up about how God cherishes us. Also, to imagine Jesus sitting with us, walking with us and talking with us. In her later life, my mother's favorite hymn was "In the Garden" … "He [Jesus] walks with me, He talks with me, He tells me I am His own." It is the imagination portion of our healing and it is good. Take Jesus with you on your next walk and *imagine* what he would say about the people you pass, the things and places you see, together.

Right now, *imagine* a time of less pain, of less heartache, of more peace.
What does that look like? What would you like to do when that *does happen?* Not *if,* but *when.* What types of things do you like to imagine? For me, when I swim at the local center, I time it so there are few people there and I can "just float." Sometimes I pray, sometimes I just talk to God and sometimes I imagine I am a SAILBOAT, the waves rock me as fellow swimmers do their laps. Or, I am on the Lake, *in* a sailboat, with sunshine and my sailing friend. I can no longer go sailing—but I have found a way to recreate the joy—even for just fifteen minutes. When done, I am rejuvenated and relaxed.

Years ago, I visited hospice patients and a dying woman told me she didn't have the patience for the noise and commercials of television so she just lay there, imagining heaven. Imagining the reunion with loved ones and what message of greeting she would have for each of them and especially beloved pets she was certain would be there to greet her. It was these "imaginings" that helped keep her blood pressure down and comforted her. She imagined sending invitations to them to greet her at "Heaven's gate." She reported that she experienced less pain when she imagined. Visualization is a powerful, therapeutic technique.

So, even while we use our intellect to figure out the Truth about ourselves and our situation, as we work to get and keep our emotions in "order" from their dis-ordered state of excessive and irrational fears, anxiety and other post-trauma symptoms, we can feel free to explore the power and peace of imagination. This also works especially well with soothing music in the background. One of my favorite music sites is in the archives of the website: www.ignatianspirituality.com or you can just Google: "Best Ignatian Songs" and listen to all the music in a variety of genre [ancient to contemporary] from a variety of artists you will recognize as well as original, sacred tunes. There is a lovely "*Anima Christi*" [Come Holy Spirit].

While we are working hard to face the "tough stuff" and win our post-trauma battles, we also deserve to treat ourselves gently, to soothe and comfort ourselves in God's love and to *imagine*, with hope and in confidence, better days ahead. It's the beautiful pictures of good imaginings that replace the bad ones we're removing. Make imagining with Jesus a part of your daily meditation.

Imagination played a key role in Ignatius' conversion. He imagined he was with the Saints doing wondrous things for God while he recuperated from his grueling surgeries. Through his years of directing the novices in the Society of Jesus, Ignatius discovered how the use of imagination can foster a deeper relationship with God.

> **Imaginative prayer is one of the hallmarks of Ignatian Spirituality.**
> **Imagination becomes another way to help us know and love God.**

Neither is it surprising that Ignatius mentions thought-oriented things in the Jesuit daily prayer of surrender—the Suscipe:

*Take, Lord, and receive all my liberty, **my memory**, **my understanding** and my entire will, all I have and call my own. Everything is yours; do with it what you will. Give me only your love and your grace; that is enough for me.*

We give our painful memories, our understanding [or lack of] to God and trust Him to receive them and work with them *for our good*. But we must voluntarily give them to Him. Now, *imagine* putting your pain in a box, taking that box-o-pain and leaving it at the foot of the Cross.

I Remember When…Memories

One of the great challenges for survivors of early and repeated childhood trauma is that many of the memories may have been repressed—boxed away by our psyche because they are too shocking for our child's mind to endure. To me, that is a perfect example of the promise: "God will not give you more than you can bear" and the reason why so many trauma survivors have memory issues.

"Some knowledge is too heavy…you cannot bear it…
your Father will carry it until you are able." Corrie Ten Boom

Other memories may have been *whitewashed* like an old picket fence to make it "look new" to the outside world, hiding the rotting wood beneath. It was so in my case. The first eighteen years were about enduring and the only way that could happen was to *not remember the worst of it;* the next twenty years were about surviving in the real world and with husband, divorce, and being a working single mom, with so many pressures and responsibilities, those memories were pushed down. They would try to surface, but were shoved back down. Like a pressure cooker with a faulty seal—the steam of those wounds seeped out here and there, scorching my heart and mind—first with confusion—"Where did *that* come from?" followed by intense shame when my angry outburst or reaction was so "over the top," it terrified my kids. I was a "screamer mom," I was a "spanker" with a short fuse.

Having had to live in terror of any and all shortfalls of perfection, and of course, there were many, I put impossible standards on my own children. Each with different temperaments, one child was compliant and obedient and thus favored. Sadly, the other child came out of the womb saying "no, no, no" to everything, defiant and stubborn and not surprisingly, bore the brunt of my wrath and brokenness. The sins of the parents—as well as their brokenness—is passed down to succeeding generations. Even without the memories, I was still running from the childhood fear of punishment that followed failure—so my pressure on them was that unconscious, kneejerk reaction…My psyche shouted, "You MUST make them obey, instantly, or something horrible will happen!" What happened was mean, unfair mom.

I went back to college at forty-eight. I'd had to give up college because of an unplanned pregnancy, a sick first child and a husband who left after a few years. It was during my undergraduate "creative non-fiction" classes that the first leaks in the pressure cooker of my memory seeped out—onto the page. All those years of reading had paid off, my vocabulary was strong and all those years of imagining gave me a descriptive uniqueness. I wrote humorous and charming essays about my early life, parents and childhood. I got great grades. One professor compared me to Eudora Welty—but they were nothing but whitewashed memories.

By 2004, as I neared graduation, my essays and poetry took on a darker edge, culminating in one entitled: "The Family Executioner" about when my mother forced eleven-year-old me to carry her dog into the vet. She not only knew the vet would put it down but told the vet, in advance, that *my* bringing the dog in was punishment for sneak-feeding the dog to literal morbid [now lethal] obesity. The vet, believing what my mother said, that I had killed this dog by over-feeding it behind my mother's back, could barely contain his anger. He lashed out in verbal condemnation, saying I didn't *ever* deserve the love of a pet [I already believed I didn't deserve the love of humans] and he hoped I would never be allowed to own a pet. The now-dead dog tumbled out of my arms onto the metal table. As I stood there, I realized for the first time my apparent function in the family dynamic: my mother's Sin-eater. It would not be the last time I served as such.

When I returned to the car she became wildly hysterical, sobbing, knowing the "deed" had been done. I sat beside her, stone-faced in shock that she would put me through that, and so blatantly lie to the veterinarian, after drilling into me "The three worst people in the world are a liar, a cheat and a thief"—unless it was a lie she told or told me to tell, or forced me to back up her lie. I realized, the more subliminal "message" was that even if I dared reveal what was happening at home, no one would believe me. This was more proof of what she always told me: "No one will ever believe you over me." I repeat, we are as sick as our secrets.

For decades, I had lived an "imaginary life." The whitewashed memories weren't my life but one I merely *thought* was mine. Then there was the life I had *actually* lived. The imaginary one in my head had angels and brothers who protected me. In reality there was a bottomless pit of anger. I was horrified to realize so much of what I believed, told and retold about my "past" was nothing but lies my mother had trained me to repeat *and* lies I told myself to "get by" to "endure." It was a lot to face until I ran across something else Corrie Ten Boom said about recovering memories:

> *"Today I know that such memories are the key, not to the past, but to the future. I know that the experiences of our lives, when we let God use them, become the mysterious and perfect preparation for the work He will give us to do."*

When we talk about our imaginations in relation to our traumatic events, especially repressed memories that come to the forefront much later in life—we also have to consider the fallacy of memory itself. Add the anxiety of potentially not being believed, or remembering, as many of us did, things that were so awful *even we* doubted their accuracy, their severity and then *accused ourselves* of perhaps blowing it out of proportion. We are overflowing with doubt. That self-doubt, amid the frequently missing pieces, mere fragments and not a cohesive "story" to be told and traced and proved, and it's understandable why so many people keep the horrors forever to themselves.

The only thing worse than never telling anyone your dark secret
is daring to tell, only to not be believed.

There is so much to be sorted, and tested, and healed. In the beginning of recovery, I was able to track down a few people who were still living, a couple public records, and a smattering of news clippings for verification—but my memories didn't come back until almost a decade *after* my mother died. There would be no opportunity to ask for explanations or her reasoning; no additional information that she might have provided would ever be found. I was left with whole years of my childhood for which I [still] had no recollection, and other years only a couple things could be retrieved. Because of the way my mother "broke me" and subsequently "re-programmed" me using psychological manipulation techniques on my then, pre-school brain, any attempts at hypnosis, brought on panic attacks followed by a hysterical meltdown that lasted for hours or days and yielded nothing. Hypnotists terrify me beyond reason.

With re-surfacing memories, one of the things my therapist and I did, was to pray *before* each session, that God would **only** bring up memories that *needed* to be dealt with, memories that were part of the "problem" for wounds that needed healing, problems that presented a barrier between me and Him and health. It gave me peace over those missing pieces. It took some of the pressure off, and now, another decade later, I don't even wonder about those missing pieces.

The reason that a therapist needs to help with repressed memories is precisely because of the potential for fallacy in memory. Ask any policeman what it's like taking witness statements after an "event." He'll likely say something like: "The culprit was tall AND short, the car was light colored AND dark colored." That's because humans "color" *every event* by our memories, our beliefs and other prejudices even if we have no conscious recollection.

During my research I found this on recovered memories: [paraphrased]

Memory is affected by **transience**—accessibility over time. Some things time doesn't mess with—others we can't remember. **Misattribution**—blatantly getting an important thing wrong. A woman reported that on the day of her divorce she left the courthouse and walked through the snow. Review of court records showed the court date was August—her misattribution was that she "FELT" bone-cold and alone. **Suggestibility**—incorporating things into your memory due to an outside influence.

Suggestibility was my greatest challenge to overcome. My mother's indoctrination techniques were intimidation and performance "reward." She intimidated me into memorizing and reciting her "script of events" so, in recovery, when asked about events that clashed with what had been discovered, I'd catch myself reciting what my mother had told me to say. [I could still hear her voice in my head]. And lastly,

Bias—remembering through the filter of our *current "feelings"* about that situation.

When I first told the story of the "Family Executioner" it created a monster that was my mother. Now, after years of therapy, reflection, research, not to mention forgiving her, the truth is not so simple.

Using the powerful tool of imagination in Spiritual Direction, I "imagined" what it was like *for my mother*, an only child, an adopted not-to-be-a-beloved-child, but as a slave. What was it like for her growing up in the house with my violent and occult-obsessed grandmother—who barged in and continued to live with Mom most of her married life. A life-altering trauma, to be sure. Then Mother had a husband and son [the aforementioned brother] who *both died on the same day*, [life altering traumas #2 & 3]. My biological father, [the subsequent husband] left her when I was an infant and my step-dad [her third spouse] who did not treat her well. It was easy to *imagine* how much she must have cherished the dog who wanted nothing from her, who wouldn't leave her and who loved her unconditionally. How badly she must have felt for having overfed the dog but to her, to say "no" was to say "You are not loved" so every nibble the dog wanted—the dog got. Imagination can help you forgive.

It was the same with her own obesity. Nowadays, we call it *comfort food*. The Bible calls it gluttony. It took me several years to get rid of the lingering anger, the "injustice of it all" because she certainly hadn't cared or even considered what it would do to my eleven year old self. But that was also *her brokenness* from *her* life-altering traumas resulting in clinical narcissism: only thinking of how something affects the "self" and others don't really enter into the consideration. But after months of trying to see *her life* from *her* eyes, and seeing how broken she was, through imagination, I was not only able to forgive her, but *imagine* her now, happily reunited with her beloved pet in heaven and the mercy of Jesus. As I did, the pain of that incident lost its power. But removing its power does not remove the scar. Even when your wounds heal, there will be scars, tender spots.

To this day, I would never own a dog, even if I could handle the walks outdoors in Michigan winters, but I have a legacy of wonderful cat friends [one at a time] who have been therapeutic, a muse and a companion. And now, having had to put a couple beloved cats "to sleep" and experience how difficult that was when I was the deeply-attached person, it reminds me of *that time* and while it doesn't excuse what she did to her child—I can have compassion for her loss.

Another word about forgiveness. It took me more than two decades to sort through all the things I needed to forgive my mother [and others] for. Maybe there's someone who's done that much "to you" in your life and you can't even think about forgiving them. A wise priest showed me how to work my way there—because although I *chose* to forgive her immediately, deliberately—forgiveness *is a process*. The priest suggested: "Until you can forgive, say this":

"Lord, I want to forgive _____, because You show so much mercy in forgiving me, but I'm not there yet. I ask You to help me forgive _____, and to open my heart so that I can. In the meantime, Lord, please forgive this person for me until I can do so for myself."

And every time, and I mean *every single time*, some past hurt pops into your mind and you feel that anger, resentment, and unforgiveness—say that powerful prayer. God will get you there, just don't give up. It will take as long as it takes and don't let anyone tell you it *should be* sooner, or instant or whatever. Make a copy and put this prayer in your Kit.

I "Feel" Your Pain...Emotions

Characteristic #2 also talks about emotions...or "feelings." Anne Frank said: "feelings can't be ignored, no matter how unjust or ungrateful they seem," and that is true. Just as true, is that our *emotions* are slaves to our *thoughts* and if we do not control them *both,* we will become a slave to our emotions. There is a dis-ordered belief that love is a "feeling." It is not. Love is a choice. What we mistake for love could be many things: hormones, fantasy, romanticism, lust, immaturity or even being "in love with love."

Love is *always* a choice, not "feeling."

The post-trauma emotions we will address here are the usual suspects: (alphabetically for all my O.C.D. friends) Anger, Fear, Depression, Disgust, Grief, Guilt, Hatred, Indignation, Rage, Resentment, Sadness, Shame, and Terror. Like love, forgiveness is not a feeling either, but a choice! I said there are only volunteers in hell. When you choose *not* to love, when you refuse to forgive—you are buying a one-way ticket!

Getting our emotions under control is a challenging task for every human, but doubly so for the traumatized soul. While our mind controls our emotions we have that pesky, overactive, adrenaline-fueled, fight-flight response to deal with; we also have those trigger-happy body memory responses. If our trauma also had a "villain" and there was no justice, there was no closure, those emotions "feel" like [there's that word again] our anger, and unforgiveness are *the only thing left* that is giving our suffering the respect it deserves. As you can well imagine, with a

If our trauma also had a "villain" and there was neither justice

nor closure, then our anger, rage and unforgiveness "feel" like

the only thing we have left to give our suffering the respect it

deserves.

hypercritical, domineering mother and a violent grandmother like mine, I had huge "women" issues, especially women who had authority over me. Not to mention the side-effect of being uncomfortable with my own femininity.   To compound the problem, I came up through the working world when women were just beginning to be placed in positions of authority. But, unlike men who usually had a mentor who took him under his wing, and mentored him into a leader, women were left to fend for themselves. So women bosses were either too soft—unable to command authority or, what I called: Hyena Management (hyenas create vicious matriarchal societies). Of course, much of what I "felt" was *my bias*, colored by the injustice and betrayal I experienced at the hands of powerful women. When you've had a trauma—whatever feelings you have near your "triggers" *will be exaggerated—dis-ordered.* They must be brought into reality. A therapist trained in P.T.S.D. is best suited for that project.

Remember I said God uses *anything and everything* to help us heal, that he sets up His plan to heal us *before* we even know we need it? While an undergrad, I worked for several years and for the first time, for not just one great woman boss, but three! I was the support person for seven Orthopaedic surgeons and their respective RN's. These women were the most amazing, professional, nurturing and mentoring women I've ever met in a workplace! I ended up leaving when it was time for graduate school because of scheduling conflicts, but I believe that God set up that experience because *He knew* "the meltdown" when the floodgates of memories opened, was on the horizon. Because I'd had such a positive experience, I was able, in therapy, to compare those women against my history of "dis-ordered" woman encounters and objectively evaluate which reactions needed to change. These women served as models of professional women worth emulating. I will be forever grateful to Sandy, Sharon and Barb!

It is normal to "have" feelings, just don't let the feelings "have" you!

For most people who've experienced a life-altering trauma, emotions are not only raw but a jumble of confusing images and impulses. While love and forgiveness are choices, there remain legitimate "feelings" of tenderness and compassion but those are often muffled by the fireworks of anger, by the ranting against injustice, the gasps of terror and whimpering cries of hopelessness.

This next Journaling Assignment is to start with the emotions *you* recognize as frequent companions and write about them. Refer to the bottom of Survey #2 if you need to. This exercise *will* stir things up. I hope, by now, that you have either/or a therapist and/or spiritual director [legally bound to silence], to help you sort out your feelings. Feelings are neither good nor, bad. They just "are." But they may be *dis-ordered* and need to be put back in order. For example, you may discover, as I did, that the item "I'm sad because" turned out to be, more often than not, ANGER turned inward. This is why a trusted, *trained* specialist can help you sort things out.

Just as we had to challenge our thoughts and "messages" about who we are, so too, do we need to challenge our emotions to find their origin. And yes, our #1 Villain remains the devil who wants control of our emotions for his own ends—to capture our souls. How many times have tragedies occurred because *feelings* of anger, rage, hatred or even depression got out of control? Murder, Road Rage, Suicide—we see the result of dis-ordered emotions every day on the news, in our streets and sadly, sometimes in our own homes.

Journaling Assignment #5:

You will start with the emotions you are feeling most often. Everyone starts somewhere different. This is for *you, for your healing,* there is no right or wrong. In the beginning, I was a rolling ball of anger and had very little sadness until later, when I realized what our mother-daughter relationship *should have been.* I grieved, not only, for the relationship I didn't have with my mother but more devastating was my grief over the relationship I didn't know how to build with my daughter. *Then the sadness was overwhelming.*

I'm Angry because: [these are general examples]

   *The guy who raped me was caught but never punished.

   *God gave me as a "gift" to parents who abused me.

   *God didn't heal me *before* I had children so I wasn't the parent they deserved.

I'm Sad because:

   *My child took their own life

   * My family died in the accident

I Feel Guilty because:

   * I was the only one in my family, group, unit that survived that tragic event.

   * I was always drunk and neglected my kids for the bottle.

Self-loathing because:

   * I had an abortion

Continue with each "feeling." It's one of those, *write until you cannot write any more.* There may be tears, you may become too upset to continue and have to stop for a bit. I was on-a-roll with Anger and sobbed my way through eight typed pages of things I was angry about! And my blessed therapist went through them all, one by one. Together we sorted, pitched and prayed many of them away. Several would take years of struggle to release. One day, one victory. Either share them with your Healer or set them aside, for now. You've worked hard! God will bless your efforts! Be pleased with yourself, do something gentle and fun—just for *you.*

A Prayer for Order

Lord, I place these dis-ordered "feelings"

At the foot of Your Cross,

Please, show me the truth and heal them

for both my spiritual growth and the health of my Soul.   *Amen.*

Am I "Crazy" or Just Catholic?

Because we've *made our way* to addressing imagination, emotions, [feelings] and intellect, and in doing so, we are challenging our *dis-ordered* ways of thinking and reacting, there's a good chance you might already have a therapist to help you deal with some psychological issues. Whether you do or not, it's time to address the difference between, and the complementarities of therapists and Spiritual Directors. For many of us, psychobabble is like speaking in tongues—confusing at best, terrifying at its worst.

As always, we look to origins to begin our exploration. Our beloved St. Ignatius, most likely a P.T.S.D. sufferer himself after his life-altering trauma at the Battle of Pamplona, was also one of the early psychologists *and* Spiritual Directors. In the literal sense of the term, as *actual* General of the Society of Jesus, his primary job was to *direct the spiritual growth* and lives of novices and govern the order. But more than that, Ignatius is one of the few saints who created a "system" for spiritual growth, a "how-to become a Saint" manual, if you will. But at the same time, he also made important discoveries about how the human psyche and soul work and what they need to heal.

Not surprisingly, many people who have experienced life-altering traumas also suffer from depression—or what they believe is depression. When I studied psychology it was years before I'd ever hear of St. Ignatius or his Spiritual Exercises. I learned about the manual for diagnosing psychological diseases and disorders or DSM, which stands for "Diagnostic and Statistical Manual" and is considered the diagnostic bible for therapists. In it, is the definition of depression begins with:

Depressed mood or a loss of interest or pleasure in daily activities for more than two weeks. Mood represents a change from the person's baseline. There was also an appendix added for a major case, often called "clinical depression" and rated the number of symptoms to meet the criteria the person must experience at least *5 of 9, present nearly every day:*

Criteria for Diagnosis of "Clinical" Depression

1. Depressed mood or irritable most of the day, nearly every day, as indicated by either subjective report (e.g., feels sad or empty) or observation made by others (e.g., appears tearful).

2. Decreased interest or pleasure in most activities, most of each day

3. Significant weight change (5%) or change in appetite

4. Change in sleep: Insomnia or hypersomnia

5. Change in activity: Psychomotor agitation or retardation

6. Fatigue or loss of energy

7. Guilt/worthlessness: Feelings of worthlessness or excessive or inappropriate guilt

8. Concentration: diminished ability to think or concentrate, or more indecisiveness

9. Suicidality: Thoughts of death or suicide, or has suicide plan

DSM – Volume V, proposed an addendum of anxiety symptoms that may indicate depression: "irrational worry, preoccupation with unpleasant worries, trouble relaxing, feeling tense, fear that something awful might happen."

NOTE: What I am about to say, by no means, implies that there are not cases of clinical depression, caused by chemical imbalances in the brain and that require medication. Not at all. Those are different and often require medication to restore balance.

However, it seems the minute someone goes to see a therapist about "depression" the *first action is to immediately* refer to a psychiatrist [that's a medical doctor who also has a degree in psychology] to get the person on "anti-depressants" *before they even want to talk to you.* You are given pills to swallow for thirty-days so that they can *get into your system* before the therapist will *begin* therapy. We were taught, in my generation, that Doctors were one step below God and if they said "swallow" these pills—you did so without question.

I wasted a decade as a pharmacological guinea pig because the original diagnosis was incorrect. How did that happen? Because I took those pills for thirty days. By the time they were *on-board*, the symptoms that would have revealed the real dis-order: P.T.S.D., were suppressed and muted. Rather, I was misdiagnosed, mislabeled and mistreated as a bi-polar all for the sake of the psychiatric version of "efficiency"…to not *waste the therapist's time* with preliminaries like me crying or being "upset" with those messy emotions of frustration and agony—after thirty days I was flat-lined emotionally.

If I had had the benefit of a longer than eight minute "here's a referral; see you in a month" un-medicated first session, [or a shrink who also looked for medical reasons— menopause and thyroid disease; *both* often present as depression] I firmly believe a skilled therapist *could* have discovered that my problems was not face-value depression. As a result, my children were raised by a woman who was three gallons of pharmacologically induced "Crazy" in a two gallon bucket—and the overflow landed on them!

Once, a *new-improved* medication had me hiding in my closet, afraid to come out because my shoes were angry at me! My poor children. I was *trying so faithfully* to get healthy. That doesn't matter, the reality was, my kids got the short end because I was fodder for some therapist's lucrative article or, to meet a quota for a kick-back from the pharmaceutical rep who sold him the drug and a busy, busy shrink who needed me to be calm and compliant.

Here's a bit of history. Those "definitions of depression" above sound all scientifically researched resplendent with *new* insights into the *modern* psyche, right? Like the never ending "new and improved" anti-depression medications endlessly hawked on the Television. The advice that "If Green Pills don't work—don't quit taking them, (that would be just common sense) just *add* the new, new, new Orange Pill!" along with the disclaimer that taking the pills may cause *new or increased symptoms or suicidal thoughts*! Isn't that what those pills were supposed to prevent in the first place?

I am *not* saying it is *never* necessary to take medication for a severe clinical depression, not at all, and certainly even hospitalization if necessary to prevent self-harm, but I am saying that catch-all diagnosis of *depression* is bandied about far too easily and medicated far too often. If you are not your *own advocate*, if you just swallow without question, you do so at your own peril. If a therapist can't give you the *time* for a correct diagnosis…run, do not walk, away.

Bluntly, the pharmaceutical companies don't care if *you* get well, they only want to make sure *your doctor* proscribes *their* pill and that *you go buy it and you KEEP taking it—for months or years.* The pharmaceutical companies don't make their gazillions unless millions of people are continuously taking their medication; so they create scenarios [massive ad campaigns] to make you believe that 1) *everyone* is depressed, 2) that everyone should be happy *all the time* and 3) taking these pills is *the only way* to make that happen. What I am saying is that the majority of people who have been convinced they are depressed are not*, but their spirit is simply and quite naturally moving quite from consolation into desolation.*

Just as the tide comes in and goes out,
Ignatius knew that our spirits move through Desolation and Consolation,
From one, into the other, and then back again.

What makes me think that? Remember those DSM V criteria for depression? They were all but plagiarized from none other than St. Ignatius, who in the 1530s identified that this human malady is not of the mind, *but the soul*. Remember, you cannot affect one part [mind] but that the other two [body & spirit] are also affected. St. Ignatius also saw this movement as the *normal* cyclical process of a human spirit. Just as there is light and dark, joy and sorrow, so too, is there Desolation and Consolation. As the tides come in and go out, Ignatius knew that our spirits move through one, into the other, and then back again. And while our mind will be *tempted* to dis-order during this time, (there's that pesky devil again) there is generally nothing "not normal" about this process. He also taught us how to deal with these movements.

Let's start with the good news: **Consolation**. It is a period of time when there is "every increase in hope, faith and charity, and all *interior joy* which calls and attracts to heavenly things and to the salvation of one's soul, quieting it and giving it *peace* in its Creator and Lord." In modern terms, it's when our prayers connect like we have God on speed-dial and He answers on the first ring. We *sense* His presence. We can say: "All is well with my soul." But it doesn't last.

Then comes **Desolation**: It is the contrary to Consolation, such as darkness of soul, disturbances in your soul, movements of things low and earthly, the unquiet of different agitations and temptations, moving to want of confidence, without hope, without love, when one finds oneself all lazy, tepid, sad, and as if separated from his Creator and Lord. Even one's thoughts are contrary to the thoughts of consolation. During this time, *it feels* like all our prayers are going to voice mail, we *cannot sense* His presence. It is then the devil swoops in and tells us we've been "unfriended" by God. That He has abandoned us. Here we are, at our weakest, being tempted by none other than the evil one himself. We feel anything but "normal." Fortunately, this doesn't last either.

> We have to remember: *This too, shall pass.*

As Ignatius wrote about the components and challenges of Consolation and Desolation, he reiterated the importance of maintaining *order in our thoughts.* What we think becomes what we say and what we say becomes what we do—and therein lies the method for making the most out of consolation and successfully enduring desolation. Being able to recognize the various movements of consolation and desolation, Ignatius called the "discernment of spirits" and it is how we know what is going on with our soul.

During the good times, as when there is a bountiful harvest we are to stock up for times of famine. Spiritually, when we are enjoying the nourishment of consolation, we are to remember—I find it helpful to journal—these wonderful feelings of connectedness, of peace. And to remember that desolation is coming and to fill our lamps against the impending darkness so that it does not catch us unaware.

When Desolation comes, there are certain things we *must do* and things we *ought never* to do. Starting with our restraints, we should *never* make a major change during Desolation, but be firm and constant in our determinations. In Consolation, it is the good spirit that guides us but in Desolation, it is the bad spirit. Therefore, it is best to make no decision. We must bear everything with *patience* for we do not know how long our desolation with last and patience is the very thing the devil will attack with all vengeance, but even in Desolation, to remember that God's grace *is* sufficient [II Cor 12:8-10] to resist *all* enemies. We cooperate with Grace when we increase those things which strengthen the soul: prayer, self-examination and by giving of ourselves more to others.

Always the kind of person who asked "Why?" I wanted to know *why* these alternating events were considered by God as good for us, what is their purpose? The example of training to be a long-distance runner came to mind. When I could barely make it around the track, I wobbled and stumbled as my weak legs grew tired. But by running around and around and around that track, my legs grew stronger so that I could run longer and longer distances before feeling the burn in my muscles. But each time I added a new mile, the burn would be back until I strengthened equal to the task. I would bask in my accomplishment, but then it would be time to add another mile. Each time, came the struggle, sometimes in breathing, sometimes in muscles, sometimes it was a bone or fall but there was *always this resistance* to my improvement. Desolation is like that.

It's no great feat to have faith when everything is going well. It's not hard to praise God when life is good and we're feeling all warm and fuzzy. But what about when we are burdened by woes that take our breath away, or stumble under the weight of our cross, or our body is wracked by endless physical pain? How much more difficult it is then? Desolation is that new extra mile, that heavier cross.

Desolation is Like That

It is a time to strengthen our spiritual muscles and there will always be resistance to improvement—but faith, perseverance and patience win the race.

Desolation is what builds our spiritual muscles like that extra mile did for my legs. Both build our stamina so we can not only finish the race, but perhaps even win it. So when God pulls back—I like to think of Him stepping behind a one-way mirror, watching us add to our strength, rooting for us, cheering us on, while knowing we have to be able to persevere, even if we don't think He's there. One of my favorite Scriptures:

"Now faith is the assurance of things hoped for, the conviction of things not seen."
[Hebrews 11:1]

Most of us will have fairly short rotations between Consolation and Desolation unless there's something special or *extra* God wants to build up in us. Most of us will not have the kind of cycle that Saint Theresa of Calcutta did.

Saint Theresa of Calcutta *knew through discernment* that God called her to form a new order and serve the homeless and dying on the streets of Calcutta. She went through various periods of Consolation and Desolation while forming her order. She recounted these in letters to her confessor through the years. But when her mission actually started, the *very day* it started, the then, Mother Theresa went into a period of desolation that lasted her entire fifty-two year ministry! That's right, Mother Theresa *faithfully* served God and the world's rejected for fifty-two years *without sensing God's presence* or the many gifts and tender mercies of Consolation. Her faith was, by then, *so great* that she could persevere on her Faith and conviction alone, that God was still with her, contrary to "feelings" and contrary to what the devil was undoubtedly saying about God having abandoned her! After she retired from active ministry, and shortly before her death, Consolation returned. Sometimes when I am hitting a bump in my own period of desolation, I think about her fifty-two years of faithfulness and I imagine Jesus greeting her and how superbly deserving she was to hear: "Well done, my good and faithful servant." I also imagine a choir of angels as back-up! That's how you become a Saint! Each of us are called to holiness.

> *Mother Theresa faithfully served God and the world's rejected for fifty-two years without sensing God's presence or the many gifts and tender mercies of Consolation.*

So while most of us, if not destined for her kind of sainthood, will not experience such long desolations, the durations will vary. The longest period of desolation I chronicled was the nine months of my "homelessness" when I had been forced to drop out of the seminary a few classes before graduation [Just like Ignatius] because my ill health devolved into permanent disability; I was unable to work and was fighting the disability red-tape, bureaucratic nightmare inherent in the Social Security system. And that's how it is sometimes, just as the world is dishing you some bitter pills, Desolation arrives, with gusto, to make it even more challenging!

In the beginning of the eighteen months following my "meltdown," when the memories were coming back with flashbacks, I had an experience that perfectly exemplifies the dangers and warnings I've just shared. So troubled by the resurfacing memories and nightmares, I failed to recognize my move into desolation. I was also having trouble sleeping and to top it all off I had a bit of a pity-party going for myself. My therapist, one of the earlier ones, showed at a lack of interest in integrating my faith with my therapy so, I enlisted the help of my parish priest. I thought that was enough to offset my therapist's disinterest. Until the day that I had an appointment with both on the same day.

During my morning appointment with Father, I mentioned my trouble sleeping and confessed to a bit of a pity-party that things were so tough in every area of my life. He recognized the onset of Desolation as the major problem. His suggestion? More prayer, perhaps a longer walk/talk after dinner, followed by reading something light, uplifting before bed, maybe journaling as many things I could be grateful for (not just 3) and to get out and do something for someone else—anonymously. That was his Prescription for what ailed me: Desolation.

Later that day, I had an appointment with the therapist—before I could put any of Father's suggestions into practice. Mr. Therapist asked me how I was doing and when I mentioned desolation he, not surprisingly, didn't know what I was talking about so I just recited my symptoms. His response? "I'm not sure what I can do for you except get you an appointment with the psychiatrist for some anti-depressants. We'll have to–*get those on board*— before we can continue." I learned two things:

> *1. It makes a huge difference what your "healers" believe religiously.*
> *2. I'm not depressed or "crazy"...I'm just Catholic!*

I left his care immediately because of this incident and kept looking until God revealed the "Angel" therapist who would help me heal. She was a Christian for sure, not certain what denomination, but we prayed before each session and her office and outer offices were full of every kind of beautiful Angel you could imagine. If you are Catholic, or you care about faith-based spiritual healing, you *must* ask the theological questions. I chose my therapist because she specialized in both P.T.S.D. and women who had been abused by their mothers *and* because she was a devout Christian. She was certainly the correct choice in helping me unearth the truth about my childhood, and make the needed behavior changes in my thinking/reasoning/responses. (Cognitive Behavioral Therapy). But knowing she couldn't give me solid **Catholic** spiritual guidance, *I had to find and add that component myself.* You must be your own advocate.

Catholics have long recognized the connection between the mind and the spirit. Many priests have training in psychology to better help parishioners navigate the combination of mental and spiritual issues. Many of the priests I've met are priests [first] but who also hold degrees in psychology as licensed therapists [second].

Before we move on the Characteristic #3, I want to emphasize that discernment of spirits, addressing Consolation and Desolation, the Examen and a life grounded in Ignatian Spirituality are so much *more* than I am able to reveal in these few pages. This is but an introduction to Ignatian Spirituality, it is a starter-kit, if you will, and only through deeper exploration and trained Spiritual Direction will you reap *all* the possible benefits. But even for those who will not continue to pursue Ignatian Spirituality as a way of progressing, these new habits will serve you and your recovery well.

Chapter Six

Characteristic #3:

Seeks to find the divine in all things, in all peoples and cultures, in all areas of study and learning, in every human experience, and (for the Christian) especially in the person of Jesus.

Characteristic #3 makes sense to any person of faith—it is basic *Imago Dei*. Seeing the "image of God" in every single human because we were all made in the image of God [Gen 1:27] and we can, with education and empathy, expand that to include other cultures, religions. By seeing the divine *in areas of study* and how knowledge benefits mankind and the planet, we become confident about achieving Characteristic #3 until we try to find the divine "in *every* human experience." For the trauma survivor, there was no divinity "there and then." In its place may be resentment that the Protector God of our childhood did *not* protect us, or worse, even allowed others we loved, to die. The echo of our screams "Where were you God? I needed you!" or that the overwhelming feeling of betrayal from that moment you realized you would not be miraculously "rescued" from the impending traumatic event. There forms a chasm, we disconnect from the God who disappointed us. There is now *dis-order* in our relationship.

Catholics proclaim the simultaneous divinity and humanity of the person of Jesus [hypostasis], so the only thing that keeps us from mastering Characteristic #3 is that hiccup regarding the difficult assignment to look for the divine <u>in</u> *every* human experience, namely, our trauma.

The Problem with Prepositions

Let's go back a moment to our foundational Scripture.

> **"Rejoice always.**
> **Pray without ceasing.**
> ***In all circumstances give thanks,***
> ***for this is the will of God for you in Christ."*** [I Thes 5:16-18]

There it is, that preposition "in" along with some pesky others. Fortunately, we have millennia of knowledge and support from our Faith's scholars and the Magisterium to correctly interpret Scripture. [Saves us from having to learn Aramaic, Hebrew, Latin *and* Greek!]

It might seem like knit-picking, but those tiny words *do* make a world of difference, especially when you are still bloody and raw from trauma and someone is asking you to be grateful. Seriously? Those prepositions can be full of trouble. Add to that some misinformed Christians who always seem eager to tell you, you are supposed to be grateful *for* all circumstances and that **those circumstances** were the will of God **for** you. As if God got up one day and said, hey, I think today a drunk driver needs to hit Sally's car and kill everyone but her and I want her to be grateful to Me **for everything**—including that!

I had a friend who believed that God specifically "willed" [selected, chose—not just allowed] all the bad in a person's life as either a punishment for their sinful, depraved heart, or to "get their attention." Sadly, she went to a church that not only preached that, but where her pastor interpreted Scriptures as he saw fit—and encouraged his flock to do the same. He felt free to change the proposition, or at least interpret it to fit his "punishing God scenario" as if God was telling us to be grateful *for* the accident that killed the family, to feel guilty and responsible for the careless actions of the drunk [If I hadn't been so sinful, God wouldn't have *made* the drunk hit us = I killed my family with my sinfulness] and the final theological error that the accident was "the will of God for you in Christ Jesus." As if God wanted that for you, individually. This kind of misunderstanding is often what happens when there is no Magisterium to clarify or when *cherry picking* [also called *proof texting*] Scripture, reduces it to pithy one-liners without historical context or comprehensive understanding in Tradition.

In relationship to our overall topic, we are working to restore order to our dis-ordered lives, just as Paul's First letter to the Thessalonians teaches them what God wants [wills] for them as a Church. Unlike Paul's other letters to other Christian communities who were in error, this letter to the Thessalonians is the first Paul writes and as instruction, lists the *attributes* of a healthy body of Christ: *rejoicing, praying without ceasing* and, like Ignatius—*to give thanks **in** all circumstances*—ending with: *"for this is the will of God for you in Christ Jesus."* [18]

So how is that to be interpreted?

First, God commits no evil so we *know with certainty* God didn't "do" that terrible thing to you. God's will is for you to be spiritually healthy, for your life to have order [and correct priorities] so that you can spend eternity with Him.

Second, that drunk chose, all on his own, [free will] to get behind the wheel of that car and drive and the chemicals in the alcohol [biology and chemistry] impaired his motor functions. I repeat: God did not "will" that evil *for you*. However, God *uses everything* that happens to you, good or bad, to reach out to you, offering an opportunity to deepen your relationship with Him.

That is God's will for each of us: a deep, intimate, relationship with Him that we might spend eternity with Him. He wills us to *rejoice,* because He's with us—through everything; *to pray without ceasing* because He knows prayer heals (us); and *to give thanks* because an attitude of gratitude banishes evil thoughts and brings us closer to Him.

Remember when we asked God to do *whatever it takes* to heal us? God will use *absolutely everything* available to heal you. And once He begins this work in us, He will never stop even if it takes the rest of our life—and most often with P.T.S.D.—it does. We have this promise from St. Paul:

> *"I am sure of this much: that He who has begun the good work in you will carry it through to completion, right up to the day of Christ Jesus."*   (Phil 1:6)

He never gives up on us. Never. Repeat that aloud: **"God *never* gives up on me!"**

So when some misinformed Christian tells you that your trauma was caused by *your* sinfulness or that you should be grateful **for** your event, you can look at them, smile gently and reply with confidence:

God's Will for Me

"I know that although God did not prevent what happened, neither did He will it [want it to happen]. Since God knows everything that will happen in the future, He knew this would happen to me and, as He promised, was not only there with me through it all, even before it happened, He began putting into place His plan to turn this evil into good. I **am** grateful for the fact that I am never alone, that God keeps His promises and that in spite of my current suffering, in the end, and because of God's grace, all will be well."

It may be a while before you can say this with *total* sincerity but it is the truth. Just like you have to repeatedly reject the bad messages about who you are; you will learn to reject bad messages about God and erroneous interpretations of Scripture and doctrine by well-meaning, but misinformed Christians.

Journaling Assignment #6

Let's re-enforce this with a letter my dear friend, Bonnie sent me. She filled in my name. So if you are reading this to help someone you love with P.T.S.D., you might want to do the same. If you are reading this for yourself… Write this out and fill in *your name.* It's a letter from God, to you, about your suffering.

My child, _____,

I loved you before you were born. I knew what your first and last words would be. I knew every difficulty you would face. I suffered each one with you. Even the ones you didn't suffer with Me. I had a plan for your life before you were born. This plan has not changed, _____, no matter what has happened or what you have done. You see, I already knew all things concerning you before I formed you. I would never allow any hurt to come into your life that I could not use for eternity, _____. Will you let me? Your truth is incomplete unless you view it against the backdrop of my Truth. Your story will forever remain half-finished…until you let Me do My half with your hurt. Let Me perfect that which concerns you.

I remain,

Your Faithful Father.

You may want to put it in your First-Aid kit. As you see, God *needs your permission* to "treat" your wounds. Please, give it.

Therefore, it is reasonable to be grateful to God for seeing you *through your trauma,* and for the other *human experiences.* God does not heal you alone. He sends His children who said "yes" to acting as His hands and feet on earth. I'm deeply grateful for the families who "adopted" me, the stranger who smiled and held the door for me that day I felt "invisible," for the "thinking of you" card from the parish card ministry, for the Mass, for Eucharist, for my gentle priest in the confessional, for my Spiritual Director when I was at seminary, for the child who forgave my motherly failings, for my friends who lift me up in prayer—human experiences one and all. The more you focus on all the positive human experiences you can be grateful *for*, the more you will be able to continue this gratitude *no matter the circumstances.* That's the goal.

> **Pope Francis:**
>
> *"Faith is not a light which scatters our darkness, but a lamp which guides our steps in the night and suffices for the journey. To those who suffer, God does not provide arguments which explain everything; rather, his response is that of an accompanying presence, a history of goodness which touches every story of suffering and opens up a ray of light."*

Before we talk a bit more about suffering, let's back up for a moment. Our ability to depend on God in the bad times, to be comforted by His Grace is directionally proportional to our trust in God, and our *trust* forms the basis of our relationship with Him. The "T" word, as in Trust is a big ask for the P.T.S.D. sufferer because our trauma shattered our world, especially if it came in the form of betrayed trust by a parent, loved one or person of authority. As always, it helps to go back to our earliest impressions and ideas and "feelings" about God and figure out where things got out of order—or *dis-ordered.*

God's in a Shoebox under the Bed

Each of us began and built our relationship with God in a unique way. I guess, I would say I've always been *God haunted*. For the first nine years of my life my total exposure to formal religion was to be dropped off at my Great Aunt Clara's on Sunday mornings by my step-dad the cop, so my Jewish mother could sleep in. Aunt Clara took me to the beautiful, white-steepled Congregational church across the street from her house. The sanctuary was on the second floor and you walked up wide, red-carpeted steps. After a couple songs, I was sent, with the other children, to Sunday school where we colored pictures of people in bathrobes. None of it made much sense to me. Afterward, I would attempt to tell Aunt Clara the story for the day and she'd correct me and then re-tell the story so that it made more sense. She'd fix us lunch and then I'd brush her waist-length strawberry red hair. I loved being with her. She took me to my first movie: The King of Kings. She had a peace about her and she spoke of Jesus with love in her voice. You knew she had a special relationship with Him.

When I got home, my step-sister would be particularly "wound up" looking for revenge that I'd gotten to go somewhere she didn't. The reason we were not both taken was because we were not oil and water, but firecracker and flame. This was the only way mom could sleep in—to have us separated. Now, I ache with sadness that my step-sister, who needed Jesus' love so desperately, had not been given a chance to meet Him back then. The poor child had been passed through my step-dad's sisters until he married my mom, but Mom had her own issues and only accepted the child because this marriage—like her others—had been a way to get out of my grandmother's house. When I got home, I was not to speak about religion. My mother, a closeted Jew who pretended to be Christian [that's a story for later] and my step-dad, a lapsed and divorced Catholic, were both on the "outs" with their respective faiths. In our house, the Word-of-the-Day from a giant dictionary perched atop an ornate podium in the dining room, replaced any "table grace" and patriotism born of their dual WWII military service, replaced religion. But I wanted to know more about God and Jesus.

I wasn't hungry or thirsty, I was ravenous.

Traveling missionaries stopped by and gave me a child's record of "Onward Christian Soldiers" and it became my instant favorite—partly because it was my only marching music, but mostly because it sang of Great deeds for God, something I wanted to do, although I had no idea what any of it really meant. I played it so relentlessly [I had many other records] that my frantic parents' complaints sounded like permission to step-sis who broke it in half. I cried for days.

Then, when I was six, my step-dad-the-cop, got shot. It was one of those incidents that I didn't realize how much I "knew" until it all came flooding back forty-two years later, in an essay. While he was in Ann Arbor fighting for his life, I was trucked off the Traverse City where cousins lived and attended the Catholic school. Loving Catholic School was the single thing my step-sister and I ever agreed on. I thought the uniforms were cool, although Mass was way too long and in Latin so it didn't make any sense but it was pretty and I loved the smell of the oil soap polish on the pews and the candlewax. It "felt" special; it looked like heaven. There is a single memory of my two-month's school attendance. It was the story of how Peter denied Jesus three times. Sister asked me how I felt about that. I stood up, stomped my buster browns and declared: "I would never, ever, deny Jesus!" That very phrase would become a catalyst for my conversion—decades later.

We moved to California when I was ten because my step-dad only had one lung left and couldn't shovel snow. Mom got a job with the space program, using her Navy teletype skills and Dad got a job in security at McDonnell Douglas where they test-fired the rocket boosters that were built at Mom's plant. It was there that Mom told me I was really "Jewish" but in the same breath that I also must not tell a single living soul. It was going to be another of our "secrets" but somehow it didn't seem as horrible as the other ones I was forced to keep.

Even though mom taught me bits and pieces about Judaism, "for our safety" she marched us down the street to the Episcopal Church on the corner every Easter and Christmas. I became quietly obsessed with God and Jews and Jesus.

I also became shameless. Once the courts had stepped in regarding my sequestered life, and I could finagle a "sleep over" at friends' houses who went to church regularly, I was doubly shameless to get invited to go with them. Using the persuasive manipulation techniques my mother used on me, and I was an apt pupil. I had a whole script that started with looking shy and saying: "Gee, Mrs. So and so…I'd sure like to know more about Jesus." Check (sleepover) and Mate (a new church to explore). During the service, I'd ask to go to the bathroom and surprisingly often, be allowed to go by myself. I'd swing through the lobby where they always had booklets and pamphlets and grab as many as I could. I'd go to the bathroom and shove them inside my clothes. When I got home, I'd pour over them and then put them in a special shoebox I'd decorated with cutout drawings from religious coloring books. I stored the shoebox, under my bed, dead-center, so if my mom found it, her very short arms would not be able to reach it, she'd hopefully lose interest and leave it alone. I fancied myself a Spy for Jesus!

At eighteen, I abandoned Jesus for Judaism. I'd been so oppressed with fear of being a Jew out-in-the-open, I decided to live openly as a Jew. But Traverse City had a tiny, sporadic Jewish community and I never really connected. By twenty, I was engaged to a Catholic boy, became pregnant and because we moved up the wedding for "respectability," I did not have time to finish the pre-cana conversion process to become Catholic like my fiancé. So my lapsed Catholic husband married his Jewish bride in the Episcopal Church. To honor my intended conversion we chose the pledge of Ruth to Naomi for our invitations and vows: "Where you go, I will go; where you lodge, I will lodge; your people shall be my people and your God my God." [Ruth: 1-16]. I always thought his people would have appreciated that—if most of them hadn't bailed on attending the wedding at the last minute, just like mine did. Soon caught up in the lives of young marrieds and with two small children, one often ill, I never got around to finishing the conversion process. We did have both children baptized in the Episcopal Church. But my husband wouldn't attend services. It was overwhelming to take two small ones by myself, so we went with door # 3—a marriage without God or religious affiliation. Predictably, within a couple years my husband realized he married me out of anger and rebellion against divorcing parents… but not love—and left.

He hated being married with endless medical bills, relentless child care and the fact he had not married for "true" love. After being counseled that if I had not yet converted, that he could divorce me and get an "easy" annulment for "defect of form," which basically said we weren't married in the eyes of the Church. So after some paperwork and a confession for *living in sin,* he would be a free man. He chose freedom. Within a year, he married a Catholic woman. They both wore white. And I got a letter from some "tribunal" that sounded, to me, like the Pope himself had declared me a harlot and my children illegitimate. Left confused and doubly heartbroken, without adequate explanation, I would avoid the Catholic Church for the next twenty years.

In Grand Rapids there was a vibrant Reform Temple and I lived openly, happily as a Jew and raised my children that way—they were, after all Jewish because their mother was. Years later, the children were confirmed at Temple Beth Israel in Jackson, Michigan. "Train children in the right way, and when old, they will not stray…" [Proverbs 22:6] Their childhood of faith-filled, joyous participation and clear identity made all the difference. My son is now president of his Temple. I gave them what I didn't have. I gave them what I could—a bloodline dating back thousands of years. But somehow, I *knew* I didn't belong there.

But on THE DAY "IT" HAPPENED, I was teaching a mid-week Temple class on "Prophets, Kings and Later Writings" while my own children were preparing for their confirmations in the next room. A student who hadn't done his homework tried to get me off topic by asking: "Is that Jesus guy really the Messiah?"

I was suddenly catapulted back to 2nd grade and that foot-stomping proclamation. "I wouldn't deny Jesus!" In returning to Judaism and the people of my blood and heritage, I had not rejected Jesus, I simply did not think of Him. We lived and worshiped *pre-Jesus.* He was never mentioned and so it was out of sight, out of mind. But on *this day,* something inside me told me that I could *not* deny Him. I was being paid to teach one thing and yet had to confess that I *did* indeed believe Jesus was the Messiah; not the political one the Jews were still looking for, but the Savior of mankind. I did what any responsible teacher would do—I faked a headache and sent everyone home. I went to see the rabbi and he said: "I thought maybe. You are the most Christian Jew I've ever met." It seems I unwittingly peppered my speech with New Testament verses! I said nothing for a couple years—gave the excuse of being sole breadwinner and exhausted, for not teaching anymore until my children left for college.

People often ask me why I left Judaism, as if there was something wrong with it. As if it lacked something. Judaism was perfect. I loved it. How could I not? I was Chosen. It is the faith of Jesus and Mary and Joseph. I enjoyed my time as part of the sisterhood. I loved the Traditions, [although you can keep gefilte fish!] the prayers, the holidays. It was *all* deeply meaningful. There was nothing, I repeat, nothing *wrong* with Judaism. I desperately miss worshipping *with* my children. Sometimes I catch myself praying in Hebrew. Although I cherish it, I will never regret leaving.

Neither did I worry about being "saved" or "unsaved" because the Jews were "Chosen." Different Covenant. God is not a liar. God does not go back on His Word. I left Judaism because of *me*. I believed *all* that Judaism taught but I believed *more*, I believed Jesus *is* the Messiah. I believed in the resurrection so leaving was my only option. I quickly rejected the Messianic Jews because I've never been much of a fence sitter. For a couple years, until the kids got out of high school and left for college, I just sat with the idea that I was, indeed, a Christian but I had no idea what "kind."

> I left Judaism because of *me*.
>
> I believed *all* that Judaism taught… but I believed *more;*
>
> I believed Jesus was the Messiah of mankind.
>
> I believed in the Resurrection.
>
> Leaving was my only option.

Once word got out that a Jew was a "free agent," there were dozens of recruitment offers and not a little pressure from some "teams" to join them. It gave me many opportunities to experience how others worship and I found it enlightening and enriching, just as I had as a child. I even hauled out the battered "Shoebox of God" I'd kept. I was hungry again.

I was pursued by aggressive evangelists, I was pressured and pummeled by Bible-thugs who see God as Punisher and all-judgment-all-the-time. Some deny the total efficacy of Baptism for the removal of original sin—but think of it more as a whitewash so God can stand to look down on us depraved beings between punishments he devises. Those were the Christians who threatened to turn me off to Christianity. I was horrified by what some churches preached—in the name of Jesus. Not the gentle Jesus of Aunt Clara's church nor the loving, brave, self-sacrificing Jesus of my cousins' Mass. One such church pressured a man who was being considered for Deacon to take himself off kidney dialysis [while he waited for a transplant] to *prove* he had *enough* faith. If he had *enough faith,* this group believed, God would heal him. So he discontinued his treatment, subsequently died, and left his wife and five children alone. I was there the day his widow got up and *thanked God* for letting him die because it convinced her God wanted her have a husband with a greater faith as guardian of her children. I can't even begin to comment on how many ways that's wrong.

In the face of such, shall we call it *diversity of belief* under the umbrella of Christianity, I knew I needed to know what *exactly* these churches stood for—or didn't. I started to study. I hated to admit it, but I am a traditionalist through and through. I was coming from a five thousand year old religion with a rich history and traditions, with miracles and first-hand encounters with the living God. I was not impressed with the "34ᵗʰ reform church of Bob," which said, to me: "If you don't like something the preacher says, leave and start your own church." I call them all *The Church of Bob.* They implied that faith and religion are about conforming God to man's desires, preferences and ambitions, rather than man to God's will.

Mainstream churches like Methodist, Presbyterian, Calvinist, Episcopalian and Lutheran had a more clear statement of belief. It was seldom clear what the "Church of Bob" believed in other than vague Christianity, interpreting the Bible as you, or Pastor Bob saw fit and shamefully, often demanding gobs of money to buy mansions, jets and TV air time. I was not impressed; I was disgusted. Further, in Judaism we had had the rabbis and scholars of the ancient writings, the commentaries and the Talmud to guide us—in addition to the Torah [law]. It was a time-earned confidence in content and scholarly interpretation. Denominations that had been around barely three-percent of the time since mankind [Hebrews] first connected with our Living God didn't seem to have the experience I needed to navigate my tumultuous life. It became clear I would be a Mainstream Christian.

Notice the list above did not include Catholic. They didn't want me, I reasoned by virtue of the cold "defect of form" annulment letter, why would I want them? I could write a whole other book about the process of ending up Catholic but suffice it to say, that in the end, I required the millennia of unbroken connection I had had in Judaism.

The deciding factor in my openness to conversion had to do with the way that my two eventual sponsors "evangelized." They didn't. Their Catholic Christianity permeated their lives. Choices they made, how they treated others, how they lived what they believed—not just Sundays but 24/7. It was "preaching the Gospel and when necessary, using words." If I asked them a question, they would answer it. Never was I made to feel stupid or pressured. I was simply "invited" to join them for Mass and for parish events where I was always made welcome. Invited. Included.

As Saint John Paul the Great said: "We evangelize by inviting, by proposing."

One sponsor was a neighbor, ten years my junior, who noticed I was alone, recovering from a leg injury and could not drive. He said he was going to church and if I wanted to go, he'd be happy to take me along. I hesitated for a couple weeks because he was Catholic. It was *that religion* where I thought the Pope had impugned my reputation and my marriage vows without knowing how sincerely, how whole-heartedly I'd made them. Finally, I agreed. I resisted all the way through Mass but couldn't help following along with great joy that it was in English and thinking back fondly to the parish in Traverse City. This parish was *versus populam* [the priest faces the parish] and when he opened his arms it felt like Jesus, Himself, was beckoning to me to come to Him. I was taken aback by the tears that welled in my eyes. When I was invited the next week, I tried not to act as eager as my heart was. There was no pressure. I had been praying and searching for a couple years by then, praying for God to show me where He wanted me. I was shocked when it became obvious, I was being called back to the Catholic Church, to keep the vow I made years ago. God had remembered my vow on the altar. He had waited for me to return and keep my promise. That's my story. What's yours?

Journaling Assignment #7:

To figure out what's wrong with a relationship you must go back to when you first met and explore how the relationship developed—or didn't.

At what age did you first start thinking about God? How did your parents and family's relationship with God or an organized religion affect you? What questions did *you* have about God? Was there anyone you could ask? Did you ever get those questions answered? If you were raised in a religion did you go along just because that was "expected" because "it's what we do" and how did you feel about that? If you could ask one question, what would you ask God? Write the history of your relationship with God, with formal religion. What do you love, what do you not like, what do you not understand? Write it all.
Maybe even write a letter *to* God.

I taught many CCD [after school Catechism] students who were there simply because it was what everyone did, what they "had to do" to get confirmed and then they could "be done" with learning about God. Sadly, that is the way many, many, children **and their parents** feel about Confirmation. Did you get confirmed? Did you know Confirmation is only *the beginning?* Did you expect and/or have a spiritual encounter with the Holy Spirit at your confirmation?

When I was preparing for my confirmation, my RCIA catechists and priest at St. Valentines in Redford, Michigan told me to fully expect the arrival of the Holy Spirit at my initiation at Easter Vigil. I accepted that without question having already experienced the sense of God's presence during prayer in both the Temple and now in my parish Sanctuary. Remember how I said God will use *anything and everything* in our lives to bring us closer to Him? God used my initiation to *prepare to* put me on the road to healing my wounds—that wouldn't be revealed for years to come.

I was initiated in 1993 and three things happened. First, during the litany of the saints our initiates knelt on the steps to the altar. I had a cast on my leg so I was a bit wobbly and I noticed, just as we sang "St. Andrew—Pray for us," one of my sponsors put his hand on my shoulder—which made me list to the other side. But as we sang "St. Ignatius *of Loyola*—Pray for us" my other sponsor leveled me out. But then they began pushing straight down, putting almost painful pressure on my shoulders to steady me—so I looked over my shoulder to mouth "OUCH!" and *BOTH sponsors were 3 feet behind me!*

Because of this incident, I began investigating St. Andrew [the namesake Cathedral I would choose when I moved to Grand Rapids and became a RCIA catechist myself] and St Ignatius *of Loyola* which led me to Ignatian Spirituality and eventual healing, decades later and ultimately—to this book. But the weird thing is that *I heard,* as clear as day: *St. Ignatius of Loyola* but what we *actually* sing in the litany of the Saints at Easter vigil is *St. Ignatius of*

Antioch!!! At my initiation I had never heard of either. It would be 23 vigils before I would actually notice it! The year I did, I laughed aloud, much to the annoyance of fellow congregants. God helped me *hear* the St. Ignatius who would help me heal! And of course, I was very proud of myself when *I discovered* St. Ignatius and Ignatian Spirituality and that I was born on the same day the Society of Jesus was formed-give or take 412 years! Ah, the times God sends us miracles and chooses to remain anonymous!

And the third thing? *The very next day,* after I had so sincerely pledged my love, devotion and *obedience* to God's will for my life—God called me on it. I received the call that my mother (yes, *that one*) was dying and if I didn't go "home" to care for her she'd be put into a former broom closet with no windows to await death because the V.A. hospital in her assigned area did not have accommodations for women. Less than 24 hours a Catholic, God asked me to go care for and ease the suffering of the woman who caused me so much pain. I went.

God, in His wisdom, helped me "do right" by my mother twelve years *before* the meltdown and recovered memories—and in doing so gave me the gift of "no regrets" by helping me care for her with compassion and that, helped pave the way to forgiveness.

Be confident, God will use *anything and everything* to help you heal, and show His love.

Our next topic—suffering, is going to be a bit of a heavy one so, before we get started, take a break and do something for yourself.

Take yourself to the movies, pick a treat from your list. I hope, by now, you are rewarding your hard work regularly. First of all, YOU have to be good to you.

God and the Mystery of *your* Suffering

So here we are, still in **Characteristic #3** and still trying to find the divine **in** our suffering. That's a big ask. When I'm suffering, all I want to do is get it to stop. I don't feel particularly holy and "getting holy" is the least of my concerns. I'm full of questions and anger and tears. The reason we discussed those pesky prepositions first, was to make sure you know, above all else: **God did not DO this to you**.

Okay, so God didn't **do** the thing that made me suffer; I'm still suffering. The drunk driver did it, the robber who shot the clerk did it, the student with the grievance and the high powered rifle—all those people, to whom God gave free will; they did it. So why do I have to pay for *their* sinfulness? You ask. "Why do," as Rabbi Kushner asked when his son died from a terrible disease, "bad things happen to good people?"

When much of my suffering happened, I was a child and my childish prayers relentlessly asked God "Why me?" Of course, as I got older I realized that the answer was "Why not me?" Seeing that *every life* contains suffering was a major breakthrough because I finally understood that I had not been [nor were you] singled out for that particular event(s), and that the correct question wasn't about *why* must I suffer but *what* do I do *with* this suffering? How do I make it stop and if I can't stop it, what then?

One conundrum was that some people (you know who they are) seem to have no tragedy in their lives while others, nothing but sorrow. The operative word there is 'seem.' Ruth Graham wrote a book and the title says it all: "In Every pew sits a Broken Heart." We don't know what another person is suffering, but in this life, everyone suffers. Everyone.

At Passover we used to sing a song "Dayenu" which means "it would have been enough" and it's about gratitude to God for the multitude of miracles and blessings bestowed on the Hebrew people to free them from slavery, sustain them through the journey and settle them in the Promised Land. Its refrain is "Dayenu"…*It would have been enough.* I used to jokingly say that song could apply to the multiple traumas visited on me during the first twenty years of my life— surely, I argued with God, "it would have been enough" for me to be given to parents who abused me physically and emotionally; surely "it would have been enough" to let some stranger attack me; surely, "it would have been enough" for me to have reproductive cancer; and so my litany of woe went on. I have Complex P.T.S.D. because several abuses were visited on my child's mind, repeatedly, over a period of time. Surely, one or even two would have, should have…*been enough*, I yelled at God. If the world were fair, but of course, it is not. Nor was it fair for children who had it far worse than I did—but I only saw my suffering.

When I got into that frame of mind, the devil chimed in with assurances that since God allowed so many bad things to happen to me I must be cursed, damned or at very least hated by the God who purportedly loved everyone equally. Surely, the devil argued, at very best, I was the proverbial "unwanted step-child of Cinderella" so why was I bothering with a God who, by virtue of all He allowed to happen to me, *obviously* didn't love me.

That devil…don't give him an inch.

Therefore, the first real question becomes: Why is there suffering? The answer: because our whole world is broken and because we each have free will. We suffer because of choices we make, we suffer because of the free-will choices others make that affect us. We suffer spiritually *and* physically. Being alive is to suffer. Just like the potty-training book: "Everybody Poops" makes something foreign and frightening to a small child more "normal." Realizing everybody suffers is the first step in facing our own suffering and ultimately the fact that everyone also dies.

Our first mistake is to try "to understand" suffering. We also want to "understand" God's reasoning behind allowing evil in the world. The devil is quick to chime in that since God made everything in the created universe He also created evil and therefore, God IS responsible for all the horrible traumatic things that have happened to you. If you succumb to this lie, it is one step from feeling picked on by God and two steps from rejecting Him for it—and the Devil wins!

Yes, God created everything, but evil is not an "original thing," as C.S. Lewis points out in *Mere Christianity,* "Evil is a parasite." For the devil to operate, he must *exist*, have *intelligence* and a *will*. Yet, existence, intelligence and will are *all good* at their origin. So evil is, as we've said again and again—a *dis-ordered* representation of something. In this case, evil is a dis-ordered good. It is good to use your God-given talents, it is evil to use them to harm others.

Dis-ordered. It is misery math: Good + a dis-ordered Will = Evil. Another explanation is that evil is the absence of good or a *lack of good*. It is something good robbed of its "goodness" and so, becomes evil. Either way, it is comforting and "understandable" for our inadequate minds to be able to say God only created good…and free will corrupted it.

In truth, suffering, like God, Himself, is a mystery.

Speaking of mysteries, the outcome of Job's trials shows clearly that the point of that whole drama, was that God is a mystery. We are mere humans. Augustine pointed out that we cannot fathom the depths of our Creator with his phrase: *Si comprehendis, non est Deus*: "If you (fully) comprehend, it is *not* God." God is incomprehensible.

In other words, God is a mystery we won't be able to crack. It's not what we want to hear. We want answers, we want to comprehend *why* we are suffering. But if we could, with our puny little human brains, fully understand all the ways of God either He wouldn't be all that much better than us, or we would be like gods. Frankly, with the complexities and fears in my life I needed a BIG God, an *omnipotent* God (unlimited authority), and a God who is *omnipresent* (always present everywhere simultaneously), that is a God I find worthy of worship and ultimately find comfort in His arms.

We Catholics, use the term: *mysterium tremendum* but the rest of that phrase more fully explains our relationship with the Divine—*et fascinans* and it means: Mystery that inspires awe and fascination. And that's pretty much it. God inspires awe for his power, and we are fascinated by this mystery we cannot unravel. In our encounters with the living God, especially in our encounters with Jesus, we get glimpses of this *mysterium tremendum* and we have to learn to be content with those. Some things we will never understand in this life. We have to accept that, no matter how difficult.

For me, the "thing" I will never understand in this life is: why God, who fully intended to heal me, who set up the how and when and where that people would arrive to help me heal, did not answer my prayer for healing *while my children were still in my care.* Why heal me now, after they have left home and one, so estranged I am all but dead to her—yet she lives a few minutes away? I loved my children with every fiber of my being, did my best (but not as good as they deserved) and prayed for healing for decades. I went from doctor, to shrink, to every self-help program on the market. I obediently swallowed pill after prescribed pill. I tried so hard. *Why heal me now, when it's too late to share my health, my life with my precious child who despises me?* I'll never know in this lifetime. I simply have to pray (daily) for acceptance. There will be things you will never know, never understand. It is the common question when a person is the "sole survivor"—why them and not me? Each of us has our own, personal, God mystery.

What's your mystery? Journal about what makes God mysterious to you.

In spite of our very individual trauma, in spite of our very personal suffering, there *is* a bit of solidarity, if not comfort, in knowing that *everyone* suffers and that *no one* has all the answers. It is never useful to compare our suffering to that of another because we can't know everything about everyone, so it is impossible to know how much others are suffering and that dooms any comparison to be skewed. The *last thing* you want to be told—in the midst of *your suffering* is to count your comparative blessings, to be grateful because so-and-so is worse off than you are. There will *always* be someone who is suffering more than you, but it is *your* suffering that you must deal with, focus on that, for now.

This reminds me of two things. First, my mother used to have a plaque on the wall that said: "I once complained I had no shoes until I met a man who had no feet." My response was "so what, my bare feet are still bloodied!" The other, is the story of the man who complains to God that his cross is too heavy to bear. God takes him to a room full of crosses of various sizes and weights and invites him to pick one that suits him better. He tries on a small one and says: "This is so light, surely I can carry more than this." Then he tries on a giant one and is crushed under its weight. And so it goes until he puts one on and says: This is the one! It's heavy enough to build up my muscles but not so heavy I can't carry it. Of course, you've already guessed, it was the one he came in with. It is true, God will not allow us to carry a cross that will crush us; if it is too heavy for us at this time, he will send a Simon (the one who helped Jesus carry His cross) to help you, until your spiritual muscles are strong enough for you and God to carry it. Remember you are never alone and if *even Jesus* needed help carrying His cross, why not you?

So, what is the *use* of suffering, its potential? Suffering can be transformed from a senseless act of a sinful other, to a saving grace (Mothers of drunk Drivers), to a cross we bear with grace *and* an opportunity to unite our suffering with Christ. As we struggle with our own cross, we connect with Jesus who also struggled with His. Just as God did not cause but *used* the betrayal of Judas, the hard hearts of the people who chose Barabbas and the violence of the Romans, to bring salvation to mankind—turning evil into ultimate good—so too, will God use *your* suffering, to bring you closer to Him and maybe for a Divine purpose, as well. It is in this way that we can find the Divine *even in our suffering*. For where we suffer, God is with us.

If the Divine Presence is with us in our suffering, and since God keeps His promise to give us grace sufficient to bear our cross, then it is now conceivable that we truly can be grateful *in all circumstances*, even in the midst of suffering. We are not grateful *for* the event, but for God's grace, presence and His promise to turn that evil into good. It is with this confidence that we can pick up our cross and carry it. We can endure, we can persevere and we can, not just survive, but thrive.

The ultimate expression of suffering, united with Christ is called "redemptive suffering." Mothers against Drunk Drivers started alcohol awareness programs so that the death of their children 'did not go to waste' but brought education so that other parents and teens might not suffer the same fate. They used their tragedy to save others. So when we suffer, we can offer it up to God for the benefit of others. We offer our pain as a living sacrifice. Is God asking you to do something with your suffering?

Chapter Seven

Characteristic #4

"Cultivates critical awareness of personal and social evil but points to God's love as more powerful than any evil."

We have now arrived at the characteristic that first caught our eye: *evil*. We've just discussed the components and origin of "evil: "Something good that God created [since He is the Author of the universe and everything in it] that has been twisted, distorted or dis-ordered from the way God created it, or used it in a way God did not intend, by *us*. By mankind. Individually, in *personal evil* and collectively, in *social evils*. We did it, we still do it. Watch the daily news. But never does the news mention the devil as our cheerleader! In the beginning of my Ignatian journey, when I got to this characteristic I made my "Innocent Victim" I.D. badge extra-large. I truly was an innocent victim as are all abused children—but that didn't mean "evil" only refers to "perpetrators" of our life-altering trauma but also to "issues" or "situations" and later in the choices we made as a result of those traumas.

Evil is frequently expressed in the twisted "excess" of something that is inherently good. Wine to make glad the hearts of men, in excess, can become alcoholism as well as domestic violence. The pleasures of this life—taken to dis-ordered excess become dark, dangerous and deadly addictions and perverse obsessions. Drugs created to restore health, to ease pain, in excess, enslave a person through addiction leading to a wasted life or even premature death. Ambition with a mission/goal, achieves great things. Excess ambition usually morphs into lethal greed, like a pharmaceutical company CEO who prices life-saving medicine out of reach of those who need it to live.

> ***"The world has enough for everyone's need, but not enough for everyone's greed."***
> ***Gandhi***

It is in situations like these that we encounter most Social evils. It is the billionaire company owner, enslaving the poor of one country, or taking jobs from Americans, to astronomically maximize profits. Or refusing to raise the minimum wage and keeping millions of Americans in abject poverty just so the executives can have a *third* home and a bigger yacht. Or government officials refusing to give the sick and elderly a cost of living raise, while they vote themselves a huge raise with unbelievable, lifetime perks. Why? It is simply because their souls are now so twisted by greed that enough is *never* enough. They have listened to the devil, they now belong to him.

Researching *social evil*, I came across a wonderful poster set up like the Periodic Table of Elements we learned in high school chemistry class. A very insightful woman named Dorothy [with website of the same name] designs many interesting things, but her Periodic Table of Social Issues is a stroke of genius.

This poster is a comprehensive encapsulation of our modern society. Of course #1 is Greed and on the opposite side at #2 is Poverty. The middle of the chart includes everything from famine to torture, from dishonesty to embezzlement, from blame and intolerance, to sexism and discord. From gluttony and waste, to corruption and tyranny. On and on, a litany of the world's woes and sins. The one thing they all have in common is that these "elements" are the "fruits," of a dis-ordered society.

> *"You will know them by their fruits...a good tree cannot bear bad fruit,*
> *nor can a bad tree bear good fruit"*   *[Matt 7: 16, 18]*

A dis-ordered *society* is the "fruit" of many, many dis-ordered souls and dis-ordered leadership. The sole job of the devil is to dis-order hearts, minds and souls—and he's good at his job. He's been doing it for a long time. And now we have the chart to show just how good!

The bottom two rows of an actual Periodic Table of Elements are normally reserved for Rare Earth and Radioactive Elements. Dorothy metaphorically records the equally-rare and precious elements as Virtues. The "radioactive" elements are right on the mark too—if the Virtues were spread globally—like radioactive fallout—then many "issues" on the above chart would be wiped out and the aftermath would, indeed, produce a very different world. Imagine if the radioactive fallout of Love and Compassion were unleashed on the world with the power of an atomic bomb!

Looking at all those social evils might be a depressing doomsday proclamation were it not for the millennia of saints, past and in-the-making, [and perhaps that includes *you*] "of good trees who bear good fruit" to counterbalance, to fight the evil. Remember, evil is a parasite. The good is here, there, everywhere; it just needs to be snatched back and protected from the devil.

Which brings us to *personal evil*. There are two parts to personal evil: the evil of the person who made us a victim and the evil we do, while blaming our victimization.

One big question for me, in light of my childhood abuse was "is a *person* ever truly evil?" or is every person good and just their "deeds" are bad? "Love the sinner, hate the sin." But growing up with daily news reports about the deeds of Charlie Manson and other horrific mass murderers, with so much emphasis on evil, vile and disgusting crimes I wondered if an evil *person* was not possible.

When I began to explore what made my mother "tick" in light of the things that were said and done, and things *she allowed to happen*, a therapist gave me the book by M. Scott Peck and his "People of the Lie" and it explained so much of my childhood—and why I was so messed up. Dr. Peck saw the "evil person" as a psychiatric diagnosis. The "evil person" isn't like the *sociopath* who does bad things but has no concept of moral conscience. Rather the evil person—or his clinical term: *Malignant Narcissism* is someone who knows *exactly* what they are doing, that it is wrong, but justifies and excuses it. Then they go to great lengths to cover it up, to make someone else "pay" for the sin [crime] so they can live in a delusional world in which they see themselves as "perfect." I wept all the way through this book as my childhood unfolded.

But, the bottom line was not what I had thought. Until Peck's book, I had been somewhat comforted thinking that Mom was "just sick and couldn't help herself but she *loved me the best she could.*" Maybe because that's what I was hoping my children would say about me. The brutal truth was that my mother was a Malignant Narcissist. To her, I was nothing more than a tool that kept her functioning, I was her Sineater and scapegoat so she could maintain her illusion of perfection. While many times in my life I have been self-absorbed to the neglect of others—I do not have her clinical diagnosis. I am capable of love and compassion. And as a Catholic, I have no delusions of perfection.

I knew, all too well, that her *version* of love was entirely *conditional* upon my performance and obedience: giving her things to brag about that made her look better. Even after I grew up and left home, my "exploits" were exaggerated and spread all over her small town. While I was the first woman admitted to the law enforcement program where I attended college and she got a great deal of mileage out of the picture of me they put on the brochure, the truth was I barely made it through with a 2.9 G.P.A. I got married and had 2 children so it took me 4 years to finish the 2-year program. While I was exceptionally accurate on the target range…I was terrified of guns, the noise and the potential violence. Years later, when I moved to mother's town to recover, post cancer surgery and divorce, she regaled my children with my DEA exploits and my undercover work. I repeated those lies, just as I had been taught. Being back in her "world" resurrected the sick, sycophant little girl who wanted to be loved so badly, who wanted approval so badly I would perpetuate any lie she told, any lie she told me to tell. The result was that years later I had to admit to my children that those were all lies. And I was left holding the bag as an adult liar who not only knew better but who had hypocritically punished *them for lying.* My children who only remembered sweet, gentle Grandma place that sin entirely on me. It's okay, they deserve a few good memories of childhood—sadly, they just don't include me. My credibility is forever destroyed with my children.

Add to that the discovery that mother was so broken that she was actually *incapable* of loving me because I was not even a human being to her, I was nothing more than her safety valve. There was no *me* as a separate being. If I continued to be like her, act like her, there would never be a separate *me.* I was in danger of my survival mechanisms turning into full-blown narcissism. Christianity is a great cure for narcissism…because it isn't about *us* but *Him*!

I don't care how old you are, finding out your mother was *incapable* of loving you, hurts. But finding out how much God loves you, heals. God's love IS enough.

My mother fit Dr. Peck's criteria of *malignant narcissism* and so did the residue I was trying to deal with. My struggles were the textbook, predictable, struggles and sufferings of children raised by such a parent. On the one hand, it was very useful for my therapist, once the core issue was identified, but on the other hand, it was horrifying to have to accept that my mother had absolutely no empathy for me, that I had truly been her Sineater because of her "absolute refusal to acknowledge her own sins." The sick, "symbiotic relationship" between us, of being named the same as her, and living as her "do over," robbed me of a child's essential sense of identity.

The perpetual "scapegoating," the "coercion and control," her unshakable "self-image of perfection," and the "intellectual deviousness"—all of it was my mother. I was left holding this giant bag of pain, grief and heartbreak—and some *very bad habits* I would have to break if I wanted to heal. I don't care how old you are, finding out your mother was incapable of loving you, hurts. But finding out how much God loves you, heals. God's love IS enough.

When I saw myself falling into the old pattern of obsequious servitude and being controlled by my mother—a pattern that I would not have a name for, for another full decade, the fight/flight of my P.T.S.D. unconscious and my motherly instinct to protect *my own children*, urged me to remove them from impending danger. I gave up my house in my hometown and took such a financial hit and forced bankruptcy that I would never, again, be able to own a home. I moved a couple of times a year after that, uprooting the children who were still angry at the move away from "fun" Grandma but I would never again feel safe *until* I had unearthed the truth—and until I surrendered my woundedness to God.

This was a long revelation of my family history, but I felt it was important to share for a couple of reasons. One is to demonstrate in a very real example that in spite of my [or anyone's] best efforts to prevent injury, others may be hurt anyway through *unintended consequences,* something many of our loved ones experience merely by close proximity to our brokenness.

Another reason for such disclosure is that neither evil nor healing happen in a vacuum. Family dynamics are often complicated and convoluted. Nothing about human relationships is the simple: White Hat Good and Black Hat Bad. Healing is messy. There will be things, choices you made, things you did, that might have been for your own protection, or simply "seemed like a good idea at the time" that turned out to be bad choices, hurtful choices, relationship destroying choices—but does that make you a bad person? No. But that does mean that at the end of the day, you too, need forgiveness.

So the question remains: Can a person *be* evil?

Are people good and the deeds the only evil thing? Has your opinion changed since the first time I asked that question? For me, I'd answer Yes *and* No. In the realm of psychological *dis-orders* [there's that disorder word again] I'd say yes, as a diagnosis, as Dr. Peck describes it, yes, evil does exist as a "type" of dis-order.

But as a Christian, I am forced to go back to that abandoned, precious *little baby* that was my mother, *before* she was adopted and broken by my equally-broken grandmother. Mom was created "good" but became dis-ordered because of her exposure to a broken, occult-dabbling, violent mother of her own.

Since that's the case, then we *also* have to go back to my grandmother's childhood as the oldest girl and primary caregiver of her nine siblings. A young woman who never had a "childhood" who was [more than once] raped by her brother, the favored first son and when she told her mother what he did, she was driven out, as a liar. Add to that Grandmother's favorite sister, Rose, the only one who showed her love, died of a disease at age nine. And you have a woman who was dealing with her own demons and brokenness. That pain led Grandmother into deep occult practices during the Age of Spiritualism. As a result of her searching for answers to her existential questions, the unintended consequence was that she exposed both my mother and I to that spiritual evil.

I spent many pre-school afternoons playing under the blanket-tent draped over the table where Grandmother spent a hefty fortune on her latest charlatan psychic. I heard the words of séances trying to connect her with dead sister Rose. There were times when I would become afraid, cold, terrified and the hairs stood on my arms. But if I cried out I would be blamed for "ruining the connection." Other times there would be nothing but pungent odors from incense. In spite of her bizarre "hobby," and what I know of Spiritual Warfare as a Christian, to heal I had to go way, back, to baby (Grandmother) Kathryn, who too, was born an innocent, precious child of God. (Original sin notwithstanding).

My family history certainly gives teeth to the twenty-four Biblical admonitions that the Lord will visit the "iniquity of the fathers" onto the third and fourth generation. In this case, it was the "mothers" of our family tree—and I was the third generation. In order to heal, I had to (and maybe you do to) look at the reasons behind someone's evil deeds *and* the reasons behind the evil of the preceding generation. Is there a pattern? In essence, I needed to heal the *whole family tree*. My own brokenness became more understandable when I came to understand both my mother and grandmother's wounds, and with understanding came compassion and the determination that this *legacy of evil* would stop with me, with my generation. Alas, it did not and my daughter ended up wounded as well.

But was it too late? Remember my question for God when I see Him? Why didn't He heal me *before* I had children; *before* I ended up with a convoluted relationship with my own children—so they didn't have to grow up tainted by my brokenness? In my fear of "becoming my mother" I held my daughter at arm's length so she wouldn't be smothered as I was, but the *unintended consequence* is that we didn't bond as we might have. Not because I didn't love her, but because I was trying to protect her from what I feared I would become. She was beautiful but I never told her because I didn't want her to become shallow and as obsessed with outward appearances as my mother had been with mine. Without realizing it, I was making my children pay for the sins of my mother-I was repeating the pattern despite my best intentions. But my daughter got hurt the worst. My son was not unscathed, but he went on to get a degree in psychology, and has a deep, steadfast faith that has helped him heal and forgive.

During the healing process and even now, from time to time, I pray the following prayer. Our parish priest has copies in the foyer of the church. So many families desperately need to heal their whole family tree.

Prayer for Healing the Family Tree
Rev. John H. Hampsch, CMF

Heavenly Father, I come before you as your child, in great need of your help. I have physical health needs, emotional needs, spiritual needs, and interpersonal needs. Many of my problems have been caused by my own failures, neglect and sinfulness, for which I humbly beg your forgiveness, Lord. But I also ask you to forgive the sins of my ancestors whose failures have left their effects on me in the form of unwanted tendencies, behavior patterns, and defects in body, mind and spirit. Heal me, Lord, of all these disorders, - pause-

With your help I sincerely forgive everyone, especially living or dead members of my family tree, who have directly offended me or my loved ones in any way, or those whose sins have resulted in our present sufferings and disorders. In the name of your divine Son Jesus, and in the power of the Holy Spirit, I ask you, Father, to deliver me and my entire family tree from the influence of the evil one. -pause-

Free all living and deceased members of my family tree, including those in adoptive relationships, and those in extended family relationships, from every contaminating form of bondage. By your loving concern for us, heavenly Father, and by the shed blood of your Precious Son Jesus, I beg you to extend your blessing to me and all my living and deceased relatives. Heal every negative effect transmitted through all past generations, and prevent such negative effects in future generations of my family tree. –pause-

I symbolically place the cross of Jesus over the head of each person in my family tree, and between each generation. I ask you to let the cleansing blood of Jesus purify the bloodlines in my family lineage. Set your protective angels to encamp around us, and permit Archangel Raphael, the patron of healing to administer your divine healing power to all of us, even in areas of genetic disability.

Give special power to our family member's guardian angels to heal protect, guide and encourage each of us in all our needs. Let your healing power be released at this very moment, and let it continue as long as your sovereignty permits.

In our family tree, Lord, replace all bondage with a holy bonding in family love. And let there be an even deeper bonding with you, Lord, by the Holy Spirit, to your Son Jesus. Let the family of the Holy Trinity pervade our family with its tender, warm, loving presence, so that our family may recognize and manifest that love in all our relationships. All of our unknown needs we include with this petition that we pray in Jesus' precious name.

Amen, Amen, and Amen.

We have "cultivated critical *awareness* of personal and social evil" in Ignatian Characteristic #4 but before we move on to the final phrase: "points to God's love as more powerful than any evil."

We still have a couple stops to make and a couple Journaling Assignments where we're going to get specific with the *social evil* of "injustice" and the *personal evils* of hatred, desire for revenge and refusal to forgive.

The Justice League

Nowadays when people think of the word "justice," they think of Law & Order, they think of "putting the bad guys away" like Dirty Harry and his .44 magnum, they think of punishment for "breaking the law" or a redress of grievances. Some might say fairness, equity.

But Justice is, more importantly, one of the four Cardinal Virtues: Prudence, *Justice,* Fortitude and Temperance. The cardinal virtues are developed and perfected through *habit.* That's right, here we are again, at our habits. Anyone can practice and achieve the four Cardinal Virtues. The virtue of Justice is most important when we have been wronged.

If we were traumatized as the result of another's actions, we may define "justice" as punishing the perpetrator equal to our own suffering—to us, *that* would be justice, that would be fair. It would be about *them* paying their debt *to us*. The courts are full of people suing to "get their due" and in many cases, that's why some laws exist—for the distribution of equality or equity—but many times the lawsuit is initiated just to soothe the rage of an exaggerated sense of entitlement. But for many of the traumatized, there is no one to "sue." You can't sue cancer, you can't sue a flood or earthquake, nor can you sue the perpetrator who was never caught. This is not to suggest that a Christian never takes anyone to court. We are members of society and we may work within the laws of our society and certainly we should seek, where possible, a reasonable redress of grievances. Those are apples, we're talking oranges.

The Justice we talk about in Spiritual Warfare is *Moral Justice*. In the Lord's Prayer, Protestants say: "And forgive us our debts *as* we forgive our debtors" while Catholics say: "And forgive us our trespasses *as* we forgive those who trespass against us." It's a tough assignment no matter which way you phrase it. It says nothing about equity. It is not designed to make the world "fair." It says nothing about us getting what is due for losses suffered.

It is about getting *us* into heaven.

I repeat, this is not to say a faithful Christian does not take legal action. Sometimes we are morally required to pursue a perpetrator, and do the scary task of testifying in court, because moral justice is about *our debt to others*. Therefore, we have a debt to, if we can, prevent someone else from suffering as we did. This was never more clearly demonstrated than in the recent courageous testimony of a young woman who had been raped. Because our society in

2017 is so morally bankrupt, it focused on discrediting the victim as not worthy of dignity or safety if she was not a virgin, and downplaying the heinousness of unwilling-sex-by-force by not calling the offender a rapist but "a superb athlete who made a twenty-minute *mistake*" (he was caught in-the-act by witnesses, as well as forensic evidence). So this young woman, put herself through being called demeaning names, in the defense's tactic to sully *her* reputation and thereby her credibility, in an attempt to increase sympathy—and leniency—for the *poor boy* who merely made *a mistake*. To everyone's horror. It worked.

As a result, the boy was let off with three months' probation, (most convicted rapists get five to seven years in prison) while the girl will struggle with the original trauma, and now the public crucifixion in the press, and on the merciless internet, as a second trauma, for many years to come. Where's the justice? Certainly not in the courts. So what do those of us who have experienced trauma at the hands of the unpunished do to get "justice?" And how can anyone mention *our debt* at a time like that? We were the victims.

Journaling Assignment #8.

Jot down in your Journal all the **painful events** you can think of when you were unfairly treated, when you were not given your "due" and especially related to your trauma. I had quite a list. Besides Mom, Stepdad and Grandma who were never "punished" by the courts for child abuse, my rapist was so mentally ill he was just returned to the mental facility, I was cheated out of a University education by parents who stole my inheritance that had been earmarked for my college education, I was cheated out of money by an unscrupulous landlord, and my list went on and on and on. Make your list now.

Journaling Assignment #9:

Before we look back on your last Journaling Assignment, and while those grievances large and small are fresh in your mind, now list all the **people** who have wronged you, hurt you, or traumatized you. Including the mean girls or bullies from school, the boy who asked you to prom and then stood you up because you dared believe someone that "cool" would notice you, the boss who fired you for something someone else did, the husband who dumped you for someone younger, all the mean, nasty, unfair, people. List them all.

Now, compare the two lists. Are there cases where there are traumas on one page and the perpetrator is on the other? Highlight those or make some sort of note because we are going to deal with those differently than the random happenings and people that are left over.

Journaling Assignment #10:

Justice is about what *we owe* and it is a Moral Virtue we can acquire through habits. Remember how we said: "forgive us our trespasses as we forgive those who trespass against us?"

Yes, I know it feels impossible when that trespasser mugged, robbed or raped us, or killed someone we love. But we're back to eating that elephant. We're going to start with a smaller bite. For this exercise, we're going to list (*for ourselves only* right now) the occasions where *our names or actions* might show up on *someone else's List #8 or #9*. For this, I want you to take the time to reach way, way, back. Did you take that extra piece of cake and let your brother get spanked for it? Even if you're an active Catholic and attend reconciliation regularly, I want you to do this exercise. Humor me. If you haven't been to confession in a while, for whatever reason, think of the "whole life" list that recovering addicts make in Alcoholics Anonymous: a list of all the people they may have wronged and to whom they need to ask for forgiveness and make amends.

Do Assignment #10 now.

Welcome back. Rest your writing hand while we take a trip back to Grammar-ville and another of those pesky prepositions. This time it is **"as"** as in: "forgive us our trespasses **as** we forgive those who trespass against us." Which means God will forgive my trespasses *in the same measure* that I forgive those who trespass against me.

Scripture makes this distinction in many places but Matthew addresses it three times. The question is always, how must *we live*, what must *we do* to get into heaven? Matthew answers.

> *"For if you forgive others their trespasses, your heavenly father will also forgive you; but if you do not forgive others, neither will your Father forgive your trespasses."*
>
> *[Matt 6:14-15]*

> *"Do not judge, so that you may not be judged. For with the judgement you made will you be judged, and the measure you give will be the measure you get."*
>
> *[Matt 7:1-2]*

And finally,

> *"Then Peter came and said to him, 'Lord, if another member of the church sins against me, how often should I forgive? As many as seven times? Jesus said to him, 'Not seven times, but, I tell you, seventy-seven times."*   *[Matt 18: 21-22]*

I know, I've never robbed a store at gun point, either, so it feels a bit lopsided forgiving something that is so much worse than anything we've ever done; it feels a bit, there's that word: *unfair*. But as Catholic Christians we know many important things about forgiveness including one that is a great comfort to us that our Protestant brethren don't have access to: Reconciliation.

As we compare our Painful Event List **8**, our Perp List **9** and our own Debt List **10,** we have an overview of all the bad things that have happened *to us* and *because of us.* We can see what others have done to us and what we have done both to ourselves and to others by way of bad choices. Although the magnitude of "sins" or "crimes" may be unequal from list to list, it's safe to say no one is free from needing forgiveness. One of the great benefits of undertaking these Journaling Assignments is that they help us put order back into our dis-ordered lives. Seeing it on the page moves us toward clarity of what, precisely, we need to deal with, and the direction we must go to *make our way* toward healing and heaven. In the terms of Spiritual Warfare, we are going to "free the captives." And right now, *we* are the bound up captive.

As always, before we "pass the broom" we're going to clean our own corner. We're going to take a gander at our *personal evil* list **10.** Ouch! That hurt. We can't euphemistically water down our responsibility for our wrongdoings by calling them "mistakes"—we need to call them what they are: sins and/or crimes. But this exercise will show us more than we might think.

First, it shows us in visual form, like that Table of Elements, where our *spiritual weaknesses* are because the honesty we strive for in Ignatian Spirituality is knowing, accepting and loving our *whole* self. Our strengths *and* our weaknesses. It also shows us our *habits*. If we have several on our list about lying, or gossiping, or drinking to excess or promiscuity, we now know *exactly* what the devil is targeting! Remember him? Yes, he was there doing the only thing he could do, whisper advice while we were deciding whether or not to do what we did. As we look at our habits, or in today's vernacular: how we are "trending," we can identify the areas that need the most work. Second, now that we know our "trends" we acknowledge that those bad habits *will* become our character if nothing is done to change them. We need to compare those choices with the type of person we want to be, the type of person God is calling us to be.

Now, please note those things you listed in Exercise #10 that you *have already confessed* in reconciliation. This might reveal a hidden problem area. If you were sincerely sorry for your sins in the confessional, there should *only* be transgressions listed *since your last confession.* This exercise was vital for me—and my confessor. I always listed my abortion—even though I was a minor child and had no control over what happened to me. Right now, please highlight those things that you *have already confessed, but listed anyway,* things that keep showing up.

These may be sins for which you have not *forgiven yourself.*

Before we look at **Journaling Assignments #8 and #9**, I want you to do two more things. Take your #10 assignment and mark all the "new sins" in one color and all the "old sins" in another. I urge you to take these lists to confession. When you're done making a good confession by addressing the "new sins," please tell Father that you also have (count them) sins you have already confessed but for which you *still* can't forgive yourself. He will help you with that.

The reason you can't forgive yourself probably has to do with your relationship with God. Perhaps you are unable to forgive yourself because you think God can only forgive, really forgive, little sins, and this one is HUGE! Or you might feel so guilty that you don't think you have been punished enough. Or it could be any number of other emotional, mental or spiritual reasons and *that* is why you need to take this to either your Confessor or your Spiritual Director. This calls for a spiritual expert. Do not attempt to do this alone at home! (Yes, God can *forgive* a contrite heart alone, from anywhere) but we're talking *healing*. There is no magic number of Journaling Assignments that can "self-help" you into dealing with *all* of this, alone. They are just concrete notes of what you need to take to an expert. Experts are experts because they know more than we do. God has also sent you an army of angels, Saints and regular folks who have said "yes" to acting as God's His hands and feet on earth. Take *all* the help you can get.

My missionary Aunt Vi and I had this conversation often. I'd say something that let her know I thought God had not, could not, forgive such-and-so. She'd ask: "Did you tell God you're sorry?" I'd answer, "Yes." and she'd finish with: "Well, then, He's thrown them into the sea of forgetfulness and you, my dear, do *not* have a fishing license." No fishing allowed!

The goal here, is that when you've looked at that list of your *debts* thoughtfully, prayerfully (otherwise known as an Examination of Conscience) and you've taken it to God in the confessional—the reality of the Sacrament of Reconciliation is, **that you walk out of that confessional completely free from sin** (all the ones you *truly repented*) **and you are then in a state of Grace.**

Therefore, you can let those "old sins" go…and if next week you were to do Journaling Assignment #10—you would *only* have a week's worth of sins to list. You need to be able to own that reality, in order to heal. **God has those sins now,** He has dealt with them and he has dealt with your Soul. You may still owe people apologies, or you may owe society a debt for breaking the laws—but YOUR SOUL IS FREE. I desperately want you to experience that release from captivity! You will no longer be a POW to sin.

Our beloved St. Ignatius' version of that #10 Journaling Assignment was a *full life* confession, and he was confessing for a couple days. If you left the Church and are now coming back, consider asking the priest to set aside enough time for you to do this. They are overjoyed to accommodate you in this regard and, especially, to welcome you home.

Every saint is a former sinner and every sinner can be a future Saint.

The difference is the single, complete, confession of a contrite heart.

Now that we have acknowledged our own sins against others, have asked for and accepted God's forgiveness, we are left with forgiving those who trespassed *against us*. **Enter the Fourth Enemy of Trauma**: our own hardened hearts, our refusal to forgive, our lust for revenge under a dis-ordered definition of "justice."

As Catholics we all know that contrition, having a contrite heart, is the key to making a good confession. We also know how the mercy of God in the case of our own sins was a healing comfort that encourages us to "mend our evil ways" because even though forgiven, we know that what God really wants is for us to live a holy life and spend eternity with Him. We also know that a contrite heart opens us up to love and makes it possible to accept God's love, as we are forgiven. So when we think about those people who have harmed us, we need to start with that open and contrite heart—yes, that vulnerable heart that is open to love. Love is a verb. Like the riddle: What has no value until it's given away? The usual answer is a smile, but it is also Love!

I have a favorite quote although I've not been able to locate the source. *"Sometimes we are called to walk open-handed among our enemies."* It had to do with what it takes to turn enemies into at very least, benign neighbors, if not friends. Someone has to be first to put down the sword. And in the situation of our trauma, it is we who are called to do precisely that.

This is what is meant by love our enemies—forgive our enemies. That doesn't mean that we have to like them, welcome them into our homes or let them spew toxicity into our lives. It doesn't mean that we don't pursue legal avenues that are open to us. I used to angrily demand: "Doesn't that mean that anyone can do *anything* to me and I *have* to forgive them or *I'm* the one risking being sent to hell?" I followed that closely with "Where's the justice in that?"

But, I was not defining *justice* as a Virtue but as retribution. I equated forgiving them with letting them "off the hook" as if that meant there were no consequences for their actions. And if they didn't have to suffer any consequences for their actions what did that make me, but a scapegoat and Sineater for someone else's evil? I'd been there; done that. It took me a long while to realize that *that is exactly what Jesus was—the scapegoat and Sineater for all of us.*

The final error of judgment in my diatribe was being "sent to hell" for not forgiving. The bottom line is that by not forgiving we are greatly reducing the measure of forgiveness to which we will be entitled. If we forgive much, much will be forgiven. That's why it is so true that there are *only* volunteers in hell. We send ourselves there, because we control how much we forgive and therefore, we control our destiny in that regard. But forgiveness, especially of big traumatic events is at once instant—our deliberate *choice* as Christians to forgive and also a *process* — bringing that choice into fruition.

The first thing to realize is that we do not forgive that person… for their benefit.

Forgiveness is not for them but for *us.* We can see now that we, ourselves, may have made all sorts of bad and harmful choices—and many of them simply because of a lack of forgiveness. bloodlust, revenge, a hardened heart—those are *our sins of unforgiveness.*

In the beginning of my adult life, I unwittingly made lots of choices based on my traumas. I entered the police academy because I saw putting the perps in jail as "justice" [that I was denied] and while it is our responsibility to protect society from repeat offenders, my motivation was darker: it was about "making them pay" and retribution. I cloaked that with the "noble" contention that I didn't want any young teen girl who was stranger-raped to be interrogated the way I had been, by chauvinistic, insensitive cops who asked what I was wearing, (implying my 1967 knee-length, baggy, Bermuda shorts were so provocative that the guy couldn't help himself, ergo it was all *my fault*), one asked if I "liked it" and the other wanted to know if I was a virgin—none of those things were relevant to what had been done to me in that violent act. But again, even my quasi-noble intent was to get *my version* of "justice" because I had been denied it. Of course, hindsight is 20/20.

Let's take a look at **Journaling Assignments #8 and #9**. We have what we could describe as minor events and major events. But surprisingly, many of the instances of "unforgiveness" are connected to minor events—minor in the grand scheme of things. Being bullied in school can have a lifelong debilitating effect. Coming in second, because the winner cheated is not such a major thing by comparison—unless it was the Olympics.

The first thing we're going to do is check out the "little things," things in assignment #8 that, now that you look at them—in comparison to the rest of your life—you think you could forgive right away. Then do the same thing with the "little people" on assignment #9. Done? Okay, let's commit them and their sins to God.

> *"Lord, these events have hurt me, and left scars on my life and on my soul. They are little grudges I carry, grudges and resentments that gave birth to prejudices against people like the ones who hurt me. Help me let go of all these hurts. I'm weary from carrying them around, they are heavy and they weigh down my soul. I give them all to You, Lord. You are true justice tempered with Mercy. I choose to forgive them and leave the rest to you."* Amen

That leaves us with the list of BIG "traumas," and the real "villains" that have us overwhelmed, that ushered in P.T.S.D., and O.C.D. and all those other things that we use to cope and try to make it through *just one more day*. The really BIG, painful stuff. It's like a forty-mile hike wearing full combat gear, in the rain and mud and heat of the jungle...and bugs. It's exhausting carrying around all of that pain. But forgiveness isn't always a one-time thing. Certainly not for survivors of prolonged captivity: POWs, women in domestic violence marriages or childhoods filled violent bullying or abuse. It's a process. Sometimes it's a long process. It's often a process that must be continually repeated. My mom said almost daily: "If at first you don't succeed, try, try, again." Who knew that that phrase, ingrained, would help me heal—from *her* actions! See, God *will* use *anything* and everything to help us heal.

After forgiving her, I can be grateful to her for saying that—and many of her other clichés—thousands of times—even though she meant it, at the time as: "until you succeed at something I can brag about to the neighbors to make me look good." God writes straight with crooked lines and being perseverant has served me well over the twenty years it took me to forgive her and others. Every time a new disturbing memory came back or I discovered another correlation between the ways she trained me, and how that was not a healthy or useful view/behavior/habit in the real world, Cognitive Behavioral Therapy helped me write a different script for my future. I was able to identify *how* I had suffered needlessly because of her "training" and how that dis-ordered habit was threatening to become my character.

I forgave her over and over and over again until I could finally let it go. And before long, when I would realize I had not *completely* forgiven her for…whatever… I'd chuckle as I said to myself and God: "If at first I don't succeed in forgiving her, let's try, try, again, Lord." I hope you will adopt this motto. Healing is messy and it doesn't happen overnight but there are delightful surprises along the way. The more you are open, the more your heart is contrite with the "right spirit" of *wanting to forgive* and *wanting to love*—then God will honor that and keep working *with you*, keep working *on you*, keep working *in you,* until it comes to fruition. Fruition: to bear fruit. So you will bear the fruit of love and forgiveness rather than the bitter fruit of hatred.

In the meantime, after you *decide to forgive, unreservedly* you can use this prayer:

> *"Lord, I know you have forgiven me many things, I know you sent your Son to die for my sins and while I have chosen to forgive _____ for _____, I'm not there yet. I want to, but my broken heart, my anger gets in the way. Please, Lord, send your Holy Spirit to help me change my heart that I may forgive completely so I can spend eternity with You. Until then Lord, please forgive _____ for me until, I can do it for myself."*
>
> *Amen*

An Indiana Jones Moment

I know, simply choosing to forgive sounds easy. It sounds more "instantly possible" than it usually is. But here, too, is how God will use *anything and everything* to help you achieve the goal you asked Him to help with. When I think about how many years it took me to forgive my mom—twenty almost, from the day of her death—I think about the turning point.

For me, the first turning point was when I became *fully committed to forgiving everyone who'd hurt me.* I was in the midst of the eighteen months of intense therapy immediately following the "meltdown" that flooded me with repressed memories. Back then, I rented lots of revenge and retribution movies and thrilled as all the bad guys got their "keesters" kicked! Afterward, I'd be depressed and full of self-pity that I didn't have a champion to "get even" for me—empty. Remember how reading about bloody battles and daring deeds left Ignatius feeling empty but, when he read about the Saints he felt encouraged, inspired to love and full of joy? Do you also remember what we learned that Ignatian Spirituality teaches us to be sensitive, to *discern* whether "low spirits" and "higher spirits" are trying to guide us? Revenge is a low spirit. The revenge path was leaving me empty—but the path of forgiveness fills you up.

Enter the only Supernatural Hero we'll ever need: God. Now, while I still enjoy martial arts films—I've opted for the Asian versions as most of them end not with retribution and revenge (even though they start out with that as the intended goal) but with repentance and/or redemption of the bad guy or by the victim's forgiveness. I'm now an aficionado of movies ending with the bad guy repenting! Father Brown Mysteries, the stories from by the great Catholic writer G.K. Chesterton are now available on video as well. Father Brown not only "gets" the bad guy, but gets them to confess and repent! Now that's a happy ending.

Buddha said: "Holding on to *anger* is like drinking poison and expecting the other person to die." Nelson Mandela substituted *resentment* for anger. I once got a misquoted fortune cooked that substituted *revenge.* Was it a coincidence that I would get *that* fortune cookie, with *that* alteration, just at the time that I was struggling with it? For days, I couldn't get that phrase out of my mind. I'd start to pray and that phrase would pop up.

Revenge is like drinking poison and expecting the other person to die.

Then, in one of my Asian martial arts films the "Master" said almost the same thing but added that the cause of the student's inability to achieve his goal was due to excessive *inner anger that had "hardened his heart."* I was dumbstruck by the timing of it all. It also became clear that I could not achieve my goal of fully forgiving *until* I did something about my anger and hardened heart. I prayed about it, I journaled about it, and puzzled over it. Yet, I still couldn't quell the anger rising up in my throat, and I couldn't soften my heart. I was bitter in the First Degree.

This went on for an agonizing week, confessing it, attending daily Mass—none of those things helped. In my dreams, the tendrils from behind my ironclad heart would attempt to strangle me. Finally, after a particularly trying day that inexplicably made me even angrier, I got into a nice hot shower to calm down but angry tears started flowing, I was praying to get rid of the anger, but I became all the more angry at God because I wasn't making any progress. I was trying and trying but what was I doing wrong?

I had been trying to soften my heart alone. It is clear now since hindsight is 20/20, that I thought *if* I followed some magic formula [and this book isn't one either], *if* I committed to some routine that I could *force* the outcome I want. That's not how it works with God; neither is it the way Ignatian Spirituality works. While this book proposes *a method* and provides a gentle guide for the journey it is still merely notes from a fellow traveler.

In the end, it is entirely about your intimate relationship with Jesus.
It's all about YOU and HIM. Period.

When I look back on it now, I can see that, at that moment, my heart was the scene of a very real epic spiritual battle. The devil was fighting *for* the hardened heart that longed for revenge, clinging to bitterness and self-pity. St. Michael was fighting him to release my heart from bondage—but as always, God needs our permission for Him to help us—and my only weapon to fight alongside St. Michael was a tough one—Complete Surrender…to God. Not just saying it, I had to *do it.*

Healing requires supernatural Grace and our cooperation with the Holy Spirit.

It was then, that I *finally* admitted to myself *and to God* that I could not do this alone—forgiving everything was SUCH A BIG ASK: to forgive all those people who had scarred me so deeply meant fighting off the devil, too—I needed God's supernatural grace. I had to *admit* I needed help, and that the only thing I could *actually do for myself* was surrender *everything* to God. Standing in that shower I cried out: "I can't unharden my heart—You have to, whatever it takes, Lord, YOU HAVE TO DO THIS!" For the first time, this control freak, actually LET GO and LET GOD.

Note: God accepts prayers whenever, wherever (the shower) and however you phrase it. He doesn't correct grammar. He reads hearts. He heals hearts. Let Him heal yours.

I no more than blurted out my surrender and it was like something out of the Indiana Jones movie where the Aztec guy reaches into a chest and plucks out the heart. I could feel a heated grasp encompassing my heart, and the sensation of something shattering. It took my breath away. I grabbed the shower railing to keep from falling. It didn't hurt exactly, but it sure didn't feel good either. I started to cry and couldn't stop. (One of my greatest fears all those years was that if I ever started to cry, I wouldn't be able to stop.) If that's your fear, I'm here to tell you: *eventually* you will stop.

After a couple days of crying until I looked like I'd gone several rounds with Sugar Ray Leonard, I was able to stop crying. But my "heavy" heart that had weighed me down, exhausted me, constricted my ability to forgive, no longer felt hopelessly burdened and that rushing undercurrent of anger that had propelled me through the first forty-five years of my life had ceased to be a raging torrent. But, neither was it a placid stream; there remained plenty of work to do—on me. I would have to repeat the forgiveness prayers, again and again. After I grew better at discernment, I could sense peace wafting over me.

But first, there must be surrender. Complete. Total. Utter. Surrender.

Sometimes I've had to "surrender" *a dozen times a day*. It doesn't mean that I wasn't sincere, it might mean the devil's poking at me in my weak spot, or that my own weak self is in need of supernatural help because I'm trying to do something outside human power.

By now, I'm sure you're wondering why I repeatedly talk about my healing struggles and at times, may give you what seems like too much information. Because I promised to be honest about brokenness, mine and especially about yours. This book was designed to be this blunt and detailed precisely because there are dozens of books out there that left me *more* discouraged and disheartened. You deserve the candid truth.

While catechetically correct, those books not only neglected *how to get started,* the author never revealed *ever* having gotten stuck and so there were no instructions for what to do when that happens. One book after another felt homogenized-by-committee editing out all *but* platitudes and regurgitations of the Catechism. The author, who had *really* been-there-done-that was also edited out. I knew I wasn't being given the whole story: that healing is messy, that I would get stuck from time to time, and that recovery is a great deal of hard work. Those books made healing sound easy, quick and complete.

My generous friends also plunked down plenty of their hard earned money with great affection and hope that maybe *that* book would have some answers. With each book, I sat, pen poised, hopeful that it would be open and honest—until it would *almost* tell me what I needed to know—like how much the devil was going to try to impede my recovery. When it didn't I'd feel betrayed and would stab the book with my pen. Much to my dismay, the holes did not help aerodynamically when I pitched it across the room.

There is nothing more blunt than Trauma,

Recovery should be honored with the same level of honesty.

I learned the Hymn, "I Surrender All" when I stayed with Aunt Vi. It is simple and mostly redundant refrain but describes *exactly* what we have to do to forgive the seemingly unforgiveable. The cost of reprinting song lyrics (copyright laws) here is prohibitive, so I suggest you check out the song on YouTube. Even the redundancy in the lyrics helps us understand we might have to keep on surrendering until we get there. And we *will*. Don't give up. It can be done. You can be free. What happens when we surrender to Him is He fills us with His Love and blessings fall on us.

Now that the remainder of **Journaling Assignments #8, #9 & #10** is down to a manageable size, there's one last thing: a Summary "to do" list. From #10, write down anyone you think you need to apologize to, or amends you need to make. From the Traumatic Events (#8), write down any of the Big Ones you need to surrender to God. Do the same with your People (#9), and the names of people you need to turn over to God, people you need to forgive. Finally, take these lists and either figuratively or literally, as I did, and place them at the foot of the Cross. [Just don't leave them there for others to see]. This is a very powerful promise to cooperate with the Holy Spirit—and it helps us remember how badly we want to heal, to feel better; to be free.

Now, look at how much smaller your battlefield is compared to when you started.

Your **Next Project:** To forgive all these remaining people and events, one by one, by first *choosing* to forgive and then by asking God to help you. When you finally do, you will be, if I may borrow from Rev. Martin Luther King Jr.: "free at last, free at last, Thank God Almighty" you'll be free at last!

This has been a very long chapter, right in the heart of the book, and for a very good reason: our wounded heart is where healing must take root and forgiveness is what heals the heart. It is in our hearts where our Spirit resides and thrives or shrivels and dies, and we must heal our spirit along with our mind and body.

By surrendering our dis-ordered desires for revenge, lingering resentments and grudges we are able to successfully deal with both social and personal evils; by choosing the path to forgiveness we are then able to finish **Characteristic #4:** *"points to God's love as more powerful than any evil."*

God forgives us mercifully for our failures. God walks with us "…through the valley of the shadow of death" (Ps 23) as we battle evil in the world and in our own hearts. He ministers to our wounds and shows us how He can write straight with crooked lines if we but surrender to Him. Ignatian Spirituality shows us how to "make our way" to Him and to health. By surrendering, we allow God to do what He does best—Love us. God *is* Love and Love is more powerful than any temporal evil, for God is eternal. What can be more powerful than eternal Love?

"There is no pit so deep, that God's love is not deeper still." Corrie ten Boom

"To believe in the crucified Son is to believe that love is present in the world and that it is more powerful than hate and violence, more powerful than all the evil in which human beings are entangled. Believing in this love means believing in mercy."

Walter Cardinal Kasper.

On my favorite Ignatian Spirituality website, (*ignatianspirituality.com),* one of my favorite contributors*,* Vinita Hampton Wright, addressed the topic of "God in the Wounds." She asks, "Can you find God in your wounds? What about the wounds of others?" With this book, we're diligently working on changing our own dis-ordered habits and healing our dis-ordered spirits but what about when we find someone in our path who is bitter and unyielding? "How is God present to the bitter?" Vinita asks. She suggests that by us, stubbornly loving that person, that person may be able to perceive God's love. Vinita reasserts what I have said, that God does not *give us* the wounds, but like her, I believe that "God is with us in our woundedness. Sometimes God's presence is disguised in the body of another person." And she prays, as I do, "to be brave enough and generous enough for God to use my very human self in just this way"

Join us in this prayer toward wholeness, won't you?

Message to Loved Ones

This is what you are doing: loving them in spite of their current bitterness, being with them in their woundedness. But, while we are healing—especially in the beginning—we wounded spirits are a major drain on those who love us. We drain you physically, emotionally, and spiritually.

You, too, are a triune being, mind, body and spirit. Please, please set healthy boundaries and avail yourself of God's great and sufficient grace as you walk with your loved one. Please attend to your own prayer life, make time to get away by yourself to recharge, you may even benefit from some counseling in healthy coping habits.

Chapter Eight

Characteristic #5
"Stresses freedom, need for discernment and responsible action."

Stresses Freedom

Ah, freedom. As American's we revere this word, we brandish this word; we live this word. We are, indeed luckier than most global citizens when it comes to freedoms that are supposedly "inalienable" and I say *supposedly* because lately the American definition of "freedom" seems to be synonymous with "Freedom to do *whatever* I want!" As in, I am *free* to kill my unborn baby. So we change our laws to make our dis-ordered desires "legal."

But for a Christian Catholic that is not the definition of freedom. Yes, God gave us free will, which means we are free to reject Him and free to choose the devil. We are free to love or not love, to do or not do…but the freedom that God gave us is the *freedom to do good* not the *license to do evil.* While our freedom includes the freedom to choose—it also makes us *free* to enjoy the consequences of our choices. Our choices matter. We are free to run up our credit card to its maximum limit buying everything we desire, but that also means we are *free* to go bankrupt, ruin our credit rating and impair our future if we are unable to pay the bill.

St. Ignatius always emphasized *deeds over words*. The actions we've taken up to now, have been *choosing* to forgive, *choosing* to develop healthy habits, and *choosing* to gently, nurture our wounded selves as we address our current pain. But what about the future? Can Ignatian Spirituality help us once we have shed the destructive baggage we've been lugging around? What can the Ignatian Principles do for us? What exactly is Characteristic #5 saying?

Characteristic #5 will be broken into three sections: Identify, Clarify and Simplify and that's how we will explore them. No doubt, by now, you recognize the word discernment from our discussion of consolation and desolation. *Discernment* will now be imbued with additional meanings, giving you excellent tools for the future.

Identify

Identify, up to now, has meant to *discover* your wounds, your weaknesses and your spiritual enemies and to identify healers and healthy practices. We used the term "discernment" as a means of identifying low or bad spirits in times of Desolation and higher or good spirits in times of Consolation. Now, we will expand our use of the word to assist us in good decision-making and to discovering [discerning] God's will for our lives, which will ultimately lead us to responsible actions.

When a person goes in for mental health therapy they are often asked in their first meeting with the therapist: "What do you hope to accomplish by coming here?" For the Life-Altering-Trauma sufferer the answer is most often: "I want to stop hurting. I want to stop being *like this!* I want more control over my thoughts, [flashbacks] life, and I want to feel whole again."

As we make our Ignatian Spiritual journey to heal our wounded souls, it is also not surprising that a common question from a Spiritual Director will be "What do you desire?" The Ignatian answer is: *id quod volo* "This I want or *Desire."* It is referring to our *deepest* desire—pure desire. We've seen how concentrated desire can go astray if not aimed in a sacred direction.

In any endeavor, you must first *identify* what you want, before you can begin to work toward it. Making this statement of desire to a Spiritual Director also comes with *the responsibility* for taking the actions necessary to *make* the desired change.

You've proven you are willing to take responsible action, by the sincere effort you have put into the journaling assignments and by continuing to make your way through this book. I've used *making our way* because we are not treating the Six Characteristics, The Examen, the Spiritual Exercises and Journaling Assignments as a destination, but rather, as a guide for our lifelong, ongoing journey. So I ask you now: what do you desire?"

Sit with that for a moment. Think about it; journal your answers. I've listed some typical answers below as a catalyst.

Together we've already identified some post-trauma *desires*:

*To put back in order that which our trauma knocked out-of-order; to quell the chaos.

*To take those re-ordered thoughts, turn them into healthy habits that sustain us in tough times.

*To gain freedom from our burdens by surrendering them to God; to experience relief.

*To make our way into the future nurtured and nourished with confidence and joy.

Pedro Arrupe S.J. [1901-1991] was one of the Superior Generals of the Society of Jesus [Jesuits] and this was his personal prayer and answer to "What do you desire?"

Grant me, O Lord, to see everything now with new eyes.
To discern and test the spirits that help me read the signs of the times,
To relish the things that are Yours and to communicate them to others.
Give me the clarity of understanding that you gave Ignatius.   Pedro Arrupe, S.J.

Identify. Clarify. Simplify.

The other thing that all Jesuits desire, and one that shows through their own decision-making-process is found in Ignatius' motto for his charges: Ad Majorem Dei Gloriam. *All for the Greater Glory of God.* Every decision, every choice we make, should *start* with our love of God and proceed from there. We know that God wants the best for us, that He wants to spend eternity with us, so the choices we make must reflect that relationship and that hope of heaven. If our choices bring the greater glory to God, we can be more sure-footed in our decisions, and more content with their outcomes.

There are three books that I want to recommend to help you learn the different facets of "discernment." Everything we do or don't do begins with a "choice." Therefore, knowing how to make the best choice possible is a high priority. Only the first book was available when I had my "meltdown" and resurgent memories, but now, for you, there is a great trifecta:

Three on Discernment

1. "The Discernment of Spirits," An Ignatian Guide for Everyday Living by Timothy M. Gallagher O.M.V. [2005].

   This one is especially helpful in understanding Consolation and Desolation.

2. "What's Your Decision?" How to make Choices with Confidence and Clarity, an Ignatian Approach to Decision Making by, J. Michael Sparough S.J., Jim Manney, and Tim Hipskind S.J. [2010].

   This one is especially helpful for decision making.

3. "God's Voice Within," The Ignatian Way to Discover God's Will, by Mark E. Thibodeaux S.J. [2010].

   This one is especially helpful for discerning God's will for your life.

The reason I insert this recommendation here is because you have made so much progress (insert grin of self-satisfaction) that you are now ready to reach out, to branch out; to seek out additional helps for yourself. It is time for you to take this basic format and customize (with the help of your healers) a recovery plan that is specific to *your needs.* In spite of the common practices here that can help anyone, you are unique and so should be your path to healing.

St. Ignatius said "It is dangerous to make everyone go forward by the same road."

This book was designed to be a hope-filled introduction, a template, if you will, for you to get the ball rolling and as you can see, **Characteristic #5**, ends with the assignment for you to take "responsible action." We are nearing a time when it will be *entirely up to you* to continue to *make your way*, to seek out help, and to maintain the healthy habits we have established here.

It is my prayer that if a certain portion of this book "speaks to you" that you will explore it further, that you will seek out related books and learn more. I want to reiterate that the Ignatian traits and practices I cover here are more of a beginner's level. Ignatian Spirituality is vast and rich and I would need a thousand pages to present all that Ignatian Spirituality is and can be. I continue to learn and gain more insight every day, every year—from these seemingly basic and simple principles. You will see in the "additional resources" section that a great many books contributed to my healing, understanding, study and research in writing this book for you.

And now…back to our program on Discernment!

One of the first things a person who has been traumatized is—*or should be*—told:

Do **not** make *any* major decisions.

When we are shocked, or grieving, or angry, we do not make sound decisions because our "decider" is dis-ordered. It is clogged with emotions, it is not rational and therefore, almost incapable of making sound, long-term decisions. From crimes of passion to road rage, our first reaction in stressful circumstances is very seldom the correct one. Sound decisions take calm.

I have often been an example of the "bad example" that proves this point. My biggest "trigger" was *not feeling safe*. For decades, I felt overwhelmingly threatened by a lurking, impending, unknown that I *was certain* would harm me, or my children. Given that, at the time, I had not yet recalled what originally made me so afraid, my mind conjured all sorts of rationalizations and justifications for making rash decisions *every time I didn't feel safe*. This was especially true if there was a sexual overtone to the *perceived* threat. While it wasn't healthy that my parents kept me sequestered in my room, my small space provided a sense of safety to it—because I could see everything in it all, at once. You can't ever see everything in real life, out in the world. I was destined for twenty years of living in, and operating from a place of fear. Even now, I will catch myself unconsciously selecting a seat with my back to the corner and then I will move to deliberately sit elsewhere, just to rejoice in that small bit of healing.

Every time I felt "unsafe" I moved. I mean, packed up my house and my kids and moved! I have actually moved my belongings fifty-nine times since I was eighteen years old. My kids went to countless schools, made and lost countless friends, deeply resented me for it and yet, I couldn't explain the compulsion to "bug out" when that fight/flight adrenaline hit my bloodstream and my "Spidey sense" screamed ALARM! FLEE! I just *knew*, deep in my bones, that we just HAD to move or something horrific would happen. To my defense, some of those times it really was "best" to move because of lecherous landlords who let themselves in with master keys or asked if I wanted to "work off" my rent. Twice I suspected drug dealer neighbors—once I was correct, the other time I wasn't. In reality, the second time, I had just suffered a *situational trauma*. I'd lost my main source of income, *and* had recently been emotionally and financially betrayed by someone very close to me. The fear became overwhelming, and I just "had to go." My poor daughter was dragged half way across the state during her last year of high school and that was monumentally unfair to her. Having me as a parent was never a picnic.

Everyone wants to make sound decisions but we, the traumatized, need even more help to do so. Many of us find our inner circle of family and friends more than eager to tell us what we *should do*, or they may even try to step in and "run our lives" since, in their opinion, we seem *so* broken we couldn't possibly do it ourselves. Help is okay, but do not give over total control—that creates an unhealthy dependency.

However, we still need to make day to day decisions. How exactly, do we do that when we're still suffering the effects of trauma? In the most basic of terms, we need to maintain our daily living—eating properly, attending to hygiene, cleaning our clothes and home, taking care of medications and other medical needs. Employment is how most of us pay our bills, but sometimes the traumatized have trouble keeping a job, or actually sitting down to pay those bills, *on time*.

Even today, I put my monthly retirement income into my checking account and the bills are all programmed to be transferred when due. I have identified that when I'm distracted or under great stress, I forget dates—and that is precisely how a great many people [especially veterans] become homeless. Flashbacks make time more fluid, they "forget" to pay the rent on time, get evicted and once evicted, it creates a snowball effect where fewer and fewer places will take a chance on a person who was evicted for non-payment of rent. If this is you, there are many ways you can arrange to make sure it doesn't happen.

My neighbor had a stroke and developed impulse issues—as in impulse internet shopping—which resulted in overdrafts and bills left unpaid and no money left for food. So she wisely had her credit union take her disability check and set the portion for fixed bills in a separate, untouchable account, so the bills would automatically be covered and paid from there. The remainder was put into an account where she could "get to" the money. It still caused issues when she bought a gadget on TV shopping network instead of groceries, but her housing and insurance and other necessities were no longer in danger. That is basic stuff.

At first, I was filled with self-loathing when I'd have to call and beg because I paid a bill late and was humiliated as "head of the household" to admit I needed help. I was ashamed that I couldn't handle that simple thing. It's all a matter of perspective. Now, I treat that option as a Perk, like having my own virtual secretary and congratulate myself for removing all bill-related stress and worry from my life. Remember, it all begins in our minds.

But what about making more drastic, more long-lasting decisions? What method could I have used when deciding whether or not to move? Many people with P.T.S.D. become/are disabled, so *when* do you decide, *how* do you decide, to sell your home and move to a more economical apartment with amenities for the disabled? Or quit a job, or accept a job outside the city? Or end a relationship? All these questions are decisions that deserve cool-headed thought, consideration and certainty because consequences for choices are real. Discernment, that's how.

For our purposes here, I offer a streamlined overview of decision-making *discernment* as outlined in the Spiritual Exercises: (Ignatius' manual for training novices)
First, try to be "indifferent," *free* of anything *keeping you from* following God's desires.

Indifference is *not* "not caring" in a mean context, but an ultimate goal. Indifference means *not preferring* one outcome over the other,

Just seeking God's Will by using the Ignatian decision-making process and *then,* being content with whatever outcome there is. The ultimate advanced Ignatian "indifference" is to not prefer health over sickness, wealth over poverty and that's because, like the Suscipe says…

"Give me only your love and your grace; that is enough for me."

That means, as long as I have God's love and grace, everything good thing is a bonus and together we can handle *any outcome.* Advanced Spirituality is being *consistently* indifferent.

Second, ask for the Holy Spirit's help. Discernment is not done on your own. Reflect on the Gospels. Make a pro and con list. As you can well imagine, the pro-con list was my O.C.D. favorite, hands down. Pray about it, but do your due diligence and put *everything* on the list. Pray some more. Tell God what you desire but as the sign in my office says:

When praying, don't give God instructions—just report for duty.

Third, weigh the various: "movements" within you to test if they are coming from God. A good indicator is that those coming from God will bring peace while the others anxiety. This is crucial for me. Knowing that my biggest trigger that causes me to make errors in judgment is FEAR, I have to be still and become acutely sensitive to whether a possible decision brings peace or anxiety. The more you practice the habits, and get to know your *whole self,* the more sensitive to the various 'movements" you will become.

Fourth, if there is no answer, rely on other practices, *imagine* what advice you would give to someone who came to you for advice. Or *imagine* what you would want to tell Jesus about this decision at the last judgment, or how you would reflect on this decision on your deathbed.

Just as we imagine Jesus defending *us* and *also* defending the person with whom we are in conflict—imagine telling Jesus about each of the possible decisions and imagine, based on the Gospels and His love for you, which He would be most pleased with. The deathbed one is amazingly helpful if you need to look at the big, long-term picture and outcome of a current decision.

Finally, after making a good discernment, *you will feel* a sense of what Ignatius calls "confirmation," or a sense of rightness. You feel in line with God's desires because you *are.*

Most of these techniques are by now, familiar but as you can see, more thought, prayer and effort goes into the decision making process than the "usual" (a) make a pro/con list and then (b) decide. That is because we also have to pay attention to which spirits [lowly or high] are pushing us and in what direction? In decision-making we must be aware, and wary, of high and low spirits to see where our inner counsel is coming from; we must make sure we are choosing wisely and with *detachment.* And we must also seek to discover God's will for us in this matter.

Clarify

Detachment, frequently used in Ignatian parlance, is somewhat interchangeable with *indifference.* While indifference is not preferring one outcome over another, detachment is both a *freedom from emotion* and a freedom from *preferring to have or not have* something. Both those words are going to be used in a new way, and in doing so will add additional meaning to *freedom,* that is more in keeping with Characteristic #5.

We have identified the decision we need to make and some of the additional steps that Ignatian Spirituality recommends to help us make a sound God-centered decision. Another important component is the removal of "emotion," eliminating the constraint of "feelings" during decision-making. Emotions can cloud our vision—removing emotions brings *clarity.*

We have all seen what road-rage does, what revenge, and other crimes of passion do when emotions and feelings are allowed free reign in the decision-making process. Just as both love and forgiveness are choices—not feelings—so too, must our decisions be free from such dis-ordered input. That is not to say we should be without empathy or compassion in our decisions, but we cannot let emotions *determine* the choices we make. We need clarity.

To that end, Ignatian Spirituality emphasizes the clarity of *detachment,* often called the "freedom of detachment." In his *First Principle and Foundation,* Ignatius talks about "making use of those things that help to bring us closer to God and leaving aside those things that don't." That is a very good definition of detachment. We detach ourselves from things that would lead us away from God; that would weaken our relationship with Him; that would let the wrong spirits influence our choices. The saints recommended, as a predisposition for prayer, "indifference." By this, they meant a willingness to move in whatever direction God is calling— especially in time of pain, crisis or discernment—to be detached—not controlled by our emotions.

Ignatius really meant it when he said we should be indifferent or detached:

> *"We ought not seek health rather than sickness, wealth rather than poverty, honor rather than dishonor, a long life rather than a short one."* **Ignatius**

That doesn't mean we shouldn't pray for health when we are sick, but we should be indifferent with the outcome. (Achieving this is Advanced Ignatian Spirituality) Certainly God doesn't will us to be sick, but if we are, if we are not instantly healed and must go through an ordeal—then it is about being okay with that, knowing, in confidence that God will turn this illness, too, for our good. It's important to remember that God always prioritizes our eternity with Him over the few years we spend on earth.

We should, instead, *desire*—there's that word again—*only* whatever God wills for our life. But how do we know when it's something we *really want?* How do we discern if it's what *He wills*, or what *we just think He wills* or, if it's just what *we want* and we put a spin on it to convince ourselves that it is what God wants? THAT is the sixty-four thousand dollar question. Learning to be comfortable with, through frequency of use, the methods of discernment we listed a few pages ago, will go a long way to help you with decisions. Don't forget to ask yourself the important question: "Which would give greater Glory to God?"

I felt the tug of resistance to the "greater glory" aspect because we are too often mislead (by the devil and misinformed Christians) to believe that devout faith, and especially the Catholic Faith with its frequent mention of the Cross, is ALL about *painful* sacrifice and denying ourselves *anything and everything* that would make us happy for the sake of duty and holiness.

We are told by the devil that God demands we *always* sacrifice every desire and including our dreams and that such a killjoy diety is not worthy of worship.

That is not the God I know and love. Nor the God Who loves me. God is my father and like a loving father He wants the very best for me *and to spend eternity with me*. But neither a loving earthly father nor our Heavenly Father will allow us to have *everything* we desire. Remember the part where God wants to spend eternity with us? Well, that means we cannot indulge dis-ordered desires—so yes, there are boundaries. Even our beloved St. Teresa of Avila ran into misinformed folks who thought holiness was a totally joyless affair as she prayed:

"From silly devotions and sour-faced saints; Good Lord, deliver us."

She knew that holiness if full of *JOY.* Many people still think a life of holiness is nothing but harsh denial, denial, denial without comfort or laughter or joy. Those embracing religious life do not see their sacrifices as harsh denials but as gifts of loving sacrifice to the Lord. Saints were some of the most joyful people ever created.

First, a sacrifice that is not made out of *loving joy* is an unworthy sacrifice and second, it is not about giving up everything that is important—but discovering what is truly important.

A sacrifice that is not made out of loving joy is an unworthy sacrifice.

As with many converts who feel "called" to the Faith, we customarily go through a phase of "What is God calling *me* to do?" after all, He called me "out" of my other religion, or from no faith, or from bad life choices, etcetera, so… WHAT NOW? More specifically, I wanted to know *what* God was calling me *to do*." Now I was, that Christian Soldier waiting to be sent into battle—just like that record I loved when I was five.

I asked my parish priest this and he laughed gently and said: "Ah, the inevitable convert question. First," he assured me, "know that Cradle Catholics [people born into the Faith] ask the same question. And I'll tell you what I tell them: God might *not* be calling you to do anything *specific*. God calls each of us, to holiness, to be a living witness and, our Sacrament of Confirmation is *the Beginning* of our call to active response—to become "Intentional Disciples" (Thank you Sherry Weddell). God wants us to *live our faith*, to use the skills we've learned and talents He gave us; to go after our dreams—and simply *Take Him Along,* every step of the way. He gave us freedom to choose, He gave us those talents to use and He wants us to be fruitful.

A book I found especially helpful in this regard is called "Forgetting ourselves on Purpose" *vocation and the ethics of ambition* by Brian J. Mahan, a Catholic layperson who teaches at Candler School of Theology, Emory University. Not surprisingly it addresses finding the answer to the universal question: what should I do with my life? What is my vocation? I love a term he coined "epiphanies of recruitment." It's that still, small voice that urges you to use your tremendous artistic (or whatever) talent even though you are being pressured to become a boiler maker, by that well-meaning parent or guidance counselor. You may still become a unionized boiler maker like your dad and provide a great life for your wife and kids—but you ALSO answer this *epiphany of recruitment* by using the art from your studio to raise money for an arts program in an impoverished school. Poet and M.D. William Carlos Williams penned beautiful poetry—between patients. What makes life meaningful is finding a way to BOTH live up to your responsibilities AND fulfill your heart's desire. Listen for that epiphany of recruitment.

Simplify

The Jesuits believe in living a *simple* life. They live uncluttered by material possessions even when they have careers outside a monastery, living simply *in all things* and sharing everything with their brothers. One Jesuit author even good naturedly lamented that a fellow Jesuit took this "sharing everything" so to heart that he found whole blocks of his own words in the other one's book—without citation!

This third part of our Identify, Clarify and *Simplify* is my favorite (okay, my O.C.D. favorite) part. We know all too well, that a life-altering trauma creates chaos from the core of our being unto the outermost reaches of our lives and relationships with others. We have struggled and worked hard to put things back in order within our minds, our hearts and even restructured our daily habits to get some sense of order *where we can* exert control, and to endure with confidence and peace *where we cannot.*

Simplicity is a path to freedom.

By praying first thing every morning, we actually *simplify* our entire day by starting it off on the right foot. But simplifying isn't just putting things in O.C.D. order, but rather simplification works *with* the detachment and indifference we learned in Characteristic #5. We simplify to get rid of *all the stuff that creates a barrier* between us and health, between us and God. It's a spring cleaning for our lifestyle, for our soul.

Just as we purged our brains of the bad messages and replaced them with God's good messages from His Holy Word, we "took the garbage out" and got rid of the clutter and dis-order in our brains and put God's Goodness In. Let's put "in" a great prayer that is perfect for right now.

Most people are familiar with the first stanza of the Serenity prayer used in the Alcoholics Anonymous program but following is the prayer, in its entirety.
Put it in your Kit.

The Serenity Prayer

God, grant me the Serenity

to accept the things I cannot change...

Courage to change the things I can,

And Wisdom to know the difference.

Living one day at a time,

Enjoying one moment at a time,

Accepting hardship as the pathway to peace.

Taking, as He did, this sinful world as it is,

not as I would have it.

Trusting that He will make all things right

if I surrender to His will.

That I may be reasonably happy in this life,

And supremely happy with Him forever in the next.

Amen.

One of the first things that helped me, was to get control over the *messy* areas of my life and my "stuff." I have never been a hoarder and if I don't use something at least once a month [except holiday specifics—like the Christmas ornaments]—I try to rid of it. But since I discovered that disability income means an even tighter budget, I started to save "just in case" stuff. If my children gave me a new appliance, I kept the old one—just in case.

During my U-Haul-Years my lack of "extras" was partly, because I moved so often that it was less to pack and partly, because, I am not a sentimentalist about "things" and had precious few "treasures." The funny thing is, I can now tell how my head clutter is doing by my house clutter. So, when I struggle with head clutter I *start* addressing it by cleaning house! But we're not talking just about housecleaning in the vacuuming, dusting sense.

First, let's talk about that actual "stuff."

Ignatius used to say if you have two coats, you're holding one that belongs to someone else. Yes, I recognize that Ignatius and all the Jesuits take a vow of poverty and wear "uniforms" and we haven't. But we can still get rid of the excess "stuff" both spiritual and physical. This is where we get to the practical part of "responsible action."

Our "time" becomes a War of Minutes

It is a matter of simple logic: there are only twenty-four hours in a day. Most Post-Trauma and P.T.S.D. people discover that they need *more time to themselves* to pray, to journal, and do the things like walks, therapy and spiritual direction *to stay* healthy. Add to that, the fact that most people have career demands, children to raise, aging parents to attend to, sick relatives/spouses, pets, church commitments, community commitments and there goes the day, the week, the year and before you know it, the decade. So our "time" becomes *a war of minutes*. A spare minute here, a spare minute there. Too often, God is put at the back of the line and gets only 'leftover' time—and by then, there isn't any. Ask my kids how they felt after only getting "tired mom, with more-work-to-do Mom, who desperately-wanted-a-nap" Last place stinks.

Conversely, what happens if you put God first and then don't have enough time to make the costume for the play, or the dinner for your spouse's boss? That certainly won't work in our hectic modern world. Remember our foundational scripture? "*Pray without ceasing*" and when combined with a bit of planning, some *simplification* around the house and multi-tasking, we can find ways to include God in everything!

Remember how I put all my financial data on "auto pilot" saving me several hours a month paying the bills, hunting for stamps and balancing the checkbook? I also have a strict budget for groceries and other needs *and* a simplified store floor plan that, using my grocery list organized –by aisle—cuts my shopping time *in half*. I can shop my four major stores, gas up the car and be back home in under three hours—with supplies for the month and some pretty hefty savings. I shop in a circle that winds back to the house using minimal gas in the vehicle. I have a divider for coupons for each store and note that on the list. I save hundreds of dollars a year as well as hundreds of hours. Hours for time with God, time to volunteer. It's a war of minutes.

Even though we didn't voluntarily take a vow of poverty, most aging and disabled people in America live well below the poverty line. It's a reality that gets worse with every price increase that is not met by a cost-of-living increase of our fixed incomes. But by the same token, there are many things I do to simplify my life, create more time, conserve precious energy, and even more precious funds, all the while allowing me to keep my priorities in the correct order. Simplicity starts with *detachment.*

My dear friend, Terry, demonstrated the perfect combination of simplicity and detachment by not being "owned" by her "things." We were having tea and I admired her teapot. She asked what mine was like and I said I used a large 6 cup glass measuring cup in the microwave. (Which, by the way, I thought was particularly clever). She immediately whipped the teapot off the table, cleaned it out, wrapped it up and GAVE IT TO ME. She saw a chance to do something wonderful for someone and took it. Frankly, I was a bit embarrassed by the worry that she might have thought I was hinting. I asked her husband why she did that and he laughed and said: "That's just her using her gift of hospitality and generosity; giving makes her happy. Terry lives *detached* from her stuff.
And I have a teapot that is now one of my "treasures."

While I have stuff, I work at not letting myself like it too much. "It's just stuff" and like the adage says: you can't take it with you! Want to know what you really value? Pretend your house is on fire, you're home alone…You have 60 seconds to grab things and get out. What do you try to save? What would you be most sad about losing? That will tell you a great deal about yourself.

"Where your treasure is, there your heart will be also."   *Matt 6:21.*

George Carlin did a very funny monologue about getting organized, getting those containers to organize all his "stuff" and then when he got it all organized he had so much room he went out and got more stuff!

It's okay to own stuff, just don't let your stuff own you.

I had the "plan" to lose enough weight to go down four sizes—the weight level where I really feel attractive and slender. However, a major orthopaedic injury and decreased lung function created a need for a steroidal medication *and* an inability to do pound-shedding aerobics. My girth swelled nearly four sizes. There was a bout of pity-eating in there too. I have my current size in the closet and the other *three* neatly boxed and labeled. Since I will, most likely, require that steroid medication for life, I needed to first *accept myself as lovable even if heavier than I would like to be.* The full serenity prayer helped… knowing the difference between what I can change and what I can't. I eat a strict diabetic diet and I swim when I can, to tone the muscles—even if I have more weight than I want. I do what I can and accept the rest.

I also needed to adopt Ignatius' idea that those other clothes *belong* to someone else. I'm getting rid of the two smallest sizes of everything. I still *have hope* and a goal to go down one size. That is realistic. Simplify. I no longer cook huge family meals so I gave all the giant cooking pots to a young mother with a growing family. Simplify. I have one of everything I "need" and a few things I "want." The bonus: I know where *everything* I own is. Imagine the time I don't waste looking for things. Okay, except for my three pairs of eyeglasses.

I gave away and/or donated twenty-two crates of books. Simplify. You would not believe the FREEDOM—how wonderful the freedom from having too many actual things *and* freedom from carrying around too many emotional things—whether burdens we need to shed at the foot of the Cross, or stuff we need to donate to St. Vincent de Paul.

When getting our physical house in order: Less is more. Then we simplify our time schedules with our *before our feet hit the floor* prayers; we cut down on expenses by being frugal; we have less laundry by donating extra clothes, less housework by having less "stuff to clean around." We create more free time by using time-saving devices and if we multi-task by praying when we cook, *and* wash dishes *and* walk the dog, we come closer to our goal of *praying without ceasing* and a real sense of accomplishment.

Undoubtedly, it's more difficult if there are other people in the house who need attention. It can get *really tough*. But you can do it! By getting rid of as many excesses as possible, it gives us a bit of control. Just as we had to unclutter our mind so that we could unclutter our heart, so now we need to take *responsible action* to declutter our physical life. I'm not saying to live like a monk in a sparse cell but ask your detached self: What power does this thing have in my life?

How much does your "stuff" cost you in time and hassle? How much of your "stuff" creates a barrier between you and God?

"The Price of anything is the amount of life you exchange for it." Henry Thoreau

Now let's talk *voluntary poverty*—the Spiritual kind.

The Lord is near to the broken-hearted and saves the crushed in spirit. *Psalm 34:18*

And in Matthew 5:3, Jesus talks about the *poor of spirit.* To the Ignatian, *spiritual poverty* is something we are *all* called to achieve.

In an excerpt from **"The Ignatian Adventure"** by Kevin O'Brien S.J.:

"All of us are called to "poverty of spirit," or *spiritual poverty*, which describes a stance of utter dependence before God, not in any demeaning, servile sense, but in the sense of the *Principle and Foundation:* God is God, and we are creatures created to praise, love, and serve God. Before all else, we depend on God for our happiness and fulfillment. While we are grateful for our talents, abilities, wealth, and achievements, we are free enough to offer them to the service of God and others and to let go of them when they get in the way of that self-giving. In short, poverty of spirit is an emptying of self so that God can fill us with life and love. Our prayer

> helps us grow in spiritual poverty and freedom.   Christ is the model of
>
> spiritual poverty *par excellence*."

Remember the prayer that the Jesuits say every day?

Suscipe

Take, Lord, and receive all my liberty,
my memory, my understanding,
and my entire will,
All I have and call my own.
You have given all to me.
To you, Lord, I return it.
Everything is yours; do with it what you will.
Give me only your love and your grace,
That is enough for me.

That is detachment.   *That* is spiritual poverty.   *That* is freedom.

And now, we move on to our final **Characteristic: #6** where it's no longer about *us* anymore, it's about what we can and are called to do *for others*.

Even in our brokenness, we have gifts worth giving, things to share.

Besides, we aren't going to be *this broken* forever and just as we are preparing for joyous days for ourselves we can look, with eager expectation to days of sharing that joy with others.

What you don't know is that dozens of people started praying for you *the moment* you opened this book to seek spiritual healing. And now, I'm asking you to join your prayers with theirs for the healing of anyone who has experienced a life-altering trauma. Pray for these anonymous souls daily, as you were prayed for.

If you are fortunate enough to make an authentic Ignatian Retreat, it will be four weeks long and mostly, silent. (Usually, only Seminarians or ordained Jesuits have that much available time!) As you will notice, we have actually undertaken many of the challenges the actual retreat presents—only ours was D-I-Y and lacked the excellent guidance of a trained Spiritual Director. But many of us will not be able to attend, afford, or experience a full retreat.

The first week, you look to gratitude for your blessings, and then at your own sinfulness and learn you are a loved sinner.

The second week, you imagine yourself with Jesus in the Gospels preaching and healing.

The third week, you explore imaginatively Jesus' passion and death and that gives you insights into suffering.

The fourth week, you explore the Resurrection and are invited into contemplation. It's called *The Contemplation to Attain Divine Love*. Which just means it's designed to help us experience God's love for us—deeply, intimately. Sadly, many people rush through this, exhausted and eager to finish up their retreat.

There is also a book called "The Fifth Week" by another of my favorite authors, William J. O'Malley, S.J. In Ignatian parlance, the *fifth week* is what Jesuits refer to as how you translate your four-week retreat experience into the rest of your life.

We are entering *the contemplation, week of our journey* through Ignatian Spirituality and it's going to begin with a great deal of thinking and journaling—but no more assignment—your journaling will be just for you, decided by you, led by the Holy Spirit.

We will begin with contemplating [thinking deeply] about how God is present in the universe, in all living creatures and nature, specifically in the newborn baby and how God works *for us*, labors *for us*, by giving us our very existence. We're going to think deeply about how things like justice, mercy, goodness and even the rays of the sun and nurturing rain all descend from God. And amongst the multitude of things for which we are grateful, we will seek total surrender, freedom and detachment. We will be able to see with new eyes, *able to see God in all things*. As you can see:

> The Six Characteristics of a person who lives Ignatian Spirituality have melded together to anchor our foundation in the Gospels, give us a constant companion in Jesus and wings to fly where the Holy Spirit will take us.

And with the Suscipe prayer, the *ideal* to want only the love and grace of God as sufficient, and although an unreachable ideal for all but a precious few, the bar must be high. Ignatius knew that and comforted us by saying that *to have the desire, for the desire, is enough* and God will do the rest.

Of the Ignatian *ideals* that we've discussed like gratitude, detachment, and discernment there is one left: *humility*. Speaking of tough assignments!

But before we move on to humility…let's do a progress report and a bit of bragging.

Where we Started…

We couldn't see any blessings because we were blinded by pain,
We couldn't feel any love because we were numbed by the violence,
We couldn't discern any balance because we were shocked by the injustice.

What we Did…

When it was time to heal, we strained to remember *any* good things, but we found them.
When it was time to write them, we even created a growing Good Book all our own.
When it was time to get the garbage out, we replaced it by putting God's Love In.

What we Learned…

We learned that finding the good requires as much courage as reciting the bad.
We learned what it is to trust, love, and feel the presence of God.
We learned that forgiveness is the step that trades surviving… for thriving.

What we Practice…

We practice daily prayer, the Examen and healthy habits for our body, mind and spirit.
We practice our Faith through the Sacraments and by giving the glory to God
We practice gratitude in all circumstances, rejoicing in confidence the Lord is with us, always.

We've come a long way, done many healing things, learned a great deal about ourselves and how God works in our lives. We've changed and grown, but we're not done yet, far from it.

It may seem contrary to human nature to be humble, to *not be* self-promoting or consumed by self-interest. It is difficult *to* indifferently *not prefer* only the "good stuff" in our life. Detachment means, being humble enough to accept *whatever* comes into our life.

Humility is being free from self-serving desires.

But, once again, being free from self-serving desires does not mean that you can't want things for yourself, or pray for things and desires of your heart, or set boundaries that protect your health and psyche. Not at all. I know, it can seem contradictory and religious double-speak but it's not.

Humility is *freedom* from the bonds of lust, greed, envy, it is the surest defense against the greatest sin of all: pride.

Equally paradoxical is the fact that there is good pride and there is bad PRIDE. Patriotism is good pride—an unjust war to impose your beliefs is bad pride. Enjoying the fruits of one's hard won accomplishments can be good pride… if it has limits. Praising your child for their achievements and mentioning it to your friends can be good pride *if* you are not doing it to make the other mothers feel that their child is *less than yours.* See that devil? Remember how the devil takes something inherently good and distorts it, makes it dis-ordered? Think about your motives. Think about where the joy of Pride comes from—genuine gladness or "I'm better than so and so."

The devil takes our *desire* to achieve and expands it into a raging lust to power and motivation for our actions; crushing people on the way up the corporate ladder. The devil also exploits our *discomfort* at being rebuked, humiliated or forgotten and turns it into a deep-seated *fear* so that when it happens we lose control, don't contain our emotions and behave rashly in response—often through revenge. The devil also distorts our relationships with others through *envy* when we want to be more…loved more, praised more, and preferred more and then evil narcissism will consume us. The devil then convinces us to take what we want because we deserve it all: Fatal Pride.

Next is a prayer that's hard to pray but so important to try, and try again. It has also been made into a beautiful song by Audrey Assad, "I Shall not Want" on her Fortunate Fall album. Check it out, it's lovely. I bought the whole album and play it often. She has a beautiful voice that delivers even more beautiful lyrics.

Litany of Humility

O' Jesus, meek and humble of heart, hear me!

From the desire of being esteemed… ***Deliver me, Jesus***

From the desire of being loved…

From the desire of being extolled…

From the desire of being honored…

From the desire of being praised…

From the desire of being preferred to others…

From the desire of being consulted…

From the desire of being approved…

From the fear of being humiliated…***Deliver me, Jesus***

From the fear of being despised…

From the fear of suffering rebukes…

From the fear of being calumniated…

From the fear of being forgotten…

From the fear of being ridiculed…

From the fear of being wronged…

From the fear of being suspected…

That others maybe loved more than I… ***Jesus grant me the grace to desire it***

That, in the opinion of the world, others may increase and I may decrease…

That others may be chosen and I set aside…

That others may be praised and I unnoticed…

That other may be preferred to me in everything…

That others may become holier than I, provided that I may become as holy as I should.

Consider putting this in your Kit.

This has been another long chapter with much to digest. We've found ways to achieve freedom by *identifying, clarifying* and *simplifying* our lives, our heads and our hearts. We have detached ourselves from dis-ordered ways of reacting and all those discoveries combined, led us to the responsible actions we must take both for our healing and in our commitment to become intentional disciples of Jesus.

Whether your *responsible action* was to keep working through this book, or finding a therapist or Spiritual Director; perhaps cleaning out the closet for St. Vincent's or cleaning out your heart for Jesus—you have made amazing progress. Please insert GOOD PRIDE! Some of the progress you can see and feel right now. You have powerful weapons to fight the enemies of your recovery. You have things you can do, right now, every day, to protect, comfort and be an active partner in your healing. You have options. You have choices and now you know how to make good ones.

Some progress will not be discernable until God is ready to show you the reflection of the *new* you, in the mirror of His Loving gaze. Many little epiphanies are on the way, many new surprises at how God will use something anyone else would consider a coincidence to let you know He is still working on you, working for you, walking beside you. Look forward to it; you have many joys ahead.

And when the not-so-great days come, and they will, because after consolation is desolation—you will know how to handle those and to Whom you should turn.

Congratulations!

You have graduated boot camp and you are now a fully-equipped Spiritual Warrior! You are now armed and ready for whatever battle comes next, and with that is your first deployment—into the world to share with others what you have learned: **Characteristic #6**

Chapter Nine

Characteristic #6

"It empowers people to become leaders in service, men and women for others, whole persons of solidarity, building a more just and humane world."

This chapter posed a problem for me, partly because it could be a brief, pithy command: "Now, go do good deeds for other people." On the other hand, it could be such a big topic with four very expandable parts. It took me a while to grasp the concept behind each clause. It's really about *the real you*, living an authentic life in and among others, and together with them, helping the world be the kind of loving, welcoming, humane world that God envisioned—and the people He encourages us to be. That is a pretty tall order. It would seem elephant is again, on the menu.

Let's start with being "real." We are the first to admit that we are not the same person we were before our traumatic event. In many ways, we are now stronger, more resilient, and the rough edges we had when we began this journey have been smoothed out some. It reminds me of my favorite passage from the children's book:

The Velveteen Rabbit by Margery Williams

"You become. It takes a long time. That's why it doesn't happen often to people who break easily, or have sharp edges or who have to be carefully kept. Generally, by the time you are Real, most of your hair has been loved off, and your eyes drop out and you get loose in your joints and very shabby. But these things don't matter at all, because once you are Real you can't be ugly, except to people who don't understand."

I used to think my woundedness made me look like that disheveled rabbit and that was, and still is, how the world sees me. I know some who do. By finding the truth about my woundedness, by learning to accept both my goodness and my weaknesses, I have become *real*. I also know that the God who so patiently loved those rough edges of anger and despair off my soul and crushed the hardened shell over my heart, will *never* cast me aside—no matter how tattered or torn. Although the world may see the loose joints and the shabbiness of that which is still unhealed, I know I am not ugly because *my* God cherishes me like the special object of a child's affection. *Each of us are loved—just as we are.*

Say that aloud: *I am loved—just as I am.*

So now that we've become real people, it is our turn to reach out to a wounded world and offer love and encouragement. I have a large collection of anonymous Jesuit prayers I clipped and saved during my recovery. The first one, of course, is surrendering to Who's really in charge—as we well know, *if* God is in charge, the devil can't be. Great news.

Dedication
Lord, Jesus, I give you my hands to do your work. I give you my feet to go your way. I give you my eyes to see as you do. I give you my tongue to speak your words. I give you my mind that you may think in me. I give you my spirit that you may pray in me. Above all, I give you my heart that you may love in me, your Father, and all humankind. I give you my whole self that you may grow in me, so that it is You, Lord Jesus, who live and work and pray in me.

To be a Person
Lord, you have made me, in your own image and likeness, in order that I should, in Christ, achieve my full stature as a person. I pray for your grace that I might become the person you would have me be. Teach me, both to understand myself and bear with myself; Grant me the grace to persevere in my efforts to become a better person, to overcome my faults, to grow in self-control, to grow in openness towards and sympathy for others. With your help may I always strive for maturity of judgment and compassion of heart, honesty in action and truthfulness in speech, Christ likeness in all things.

To be Unselfish
Lord, Jesus; in your life you showed me the example of love for others. Free me from thinking about myself all the time or putting me first. Teach me; how a heart that loves others is happier than a heart that may say: "Me First." Teach me; How to find joy in helping others and how to give without expecting something in return, to keep the thought of your own unselfish life always before me.

That's right, we've come to the part of our journey where we realize that "It's not about me." I've mentioned several times that although I shared stories of *my* healing journey—in the end, it was *never about me.* And while your trauma happened *to you*—it isn't exclusively about *you* either. It is about God, Jesus, the Holy Spirit and our relationship with the divine.

Characteristic #6 "empowers people to become leaders in service."

Mothers Against Drunk Drivers, became leaders of information and change, just as the survivors of other traumas reach out to those newly traumatized. The **Wounded Warriors Program** where amputees mentor the growing number of veterans who face the many life changes after amputation. **The Rachael Project** is for post abortion recovery. Sponsors in **Alcoholics and Narcotics Anonymous** help those in recovery take it one day at a time. Just to name a few. When we take our pain and hard-learned lessons and use them to lift others up, we receive a healing balm in alleviating another's pain. This balm is Grace from a Savior who says: "As you do unto the least of these, you do unto me."

You simply cannot out-give God.
The more you give, the more He will multiply your *joy*.

The picture below is the only picture in this book.

The vase was obviously dropped, broken and not-so-perfectly put back together. It even has pieces missing. There's a gaping hole that, at first glance, makes this otherwise stunning piece of pottery seem useless and ugly. What do you think? Would you keep it?

I affectionately call it my "Self-Portrait." When I first started recovery that's how I felt:

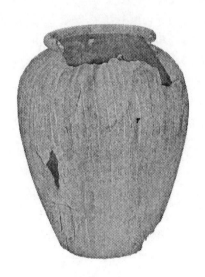

irreparably broken, useless and ugly. I lamented that I would never be "whole" again. And while I was correct, that I am not my former "wholeness," and will probably never be in this lifetime, I now realize that this broken, mostly-repaired version of myself is actually better. All the anger that broke it against the hardness of my heart is gone; the pain of being "in pieces" has been restored by none other than the Hand of the Master Craftsman, and even if my brokenness *is* more visible to the outside world than my previous "pretended wholeness" was—I am a better vase, a more beautiful vase and a vase more useful to God and others than I ever was before.

Now look closely. The Master Craftsman left it solid enough to hold *just enough* water to nourish beautiful flowers. So when I give myself, to capacity, I *can* hold and nurture a huge bouquet of beautiful flowers—my gift to others—and those flowers will cover most of my cracks.

God isn't finished healing me, *or you,* He will continue until He finishes the work he started within us. In the meantime, the more we do for others, the more God will use our devotion and offerings to enrich the healing process, bringing meaning and *joy.* So much joy into our lives, it deserves all caps: JOY!

Our parish offered the "Called and Gifted" program from the St. Catherine of Siena Institute and Sherry Weddell. It teaches us to discern our *skills* [something that can be taught], our *talents* [given by God] and our *charisms* [special gift/talent/service that we joyfully give *back to God*]. The idea is that *after* we know which of our gifts fall into which category, we can better become "Intentional Disciples" and take action in both our Faith community and the world at large. It's not unlike our discernment of God's will but it puts the emphasis on *us* deciding what to do with the many gifts and blessings we have been given and that we are now aware of. It also offers more of that freedom we learned about earlier.

I've always had an affinity for numbers. I hold a Master's in business and have many years' experience in bookkeeping, so whenever there was a need for someone in the parish to deal with finances, fundraising, etc. I felt obligated to use my *skill*, to say "yes" and I felt guilty if I said "no." I dreaded being asked, didn't enjoy the work—it just felt like more work that I did during the week. I was not a cheerful giver. Then I took this program. I realized that accounting was a skill but writing, storytelling and organizing are my *talents* and that Catechesis—teaching the Catholic Faith—is one of my *charisms.*

Charism, "How do you know?" I asked. It's something that you do *just for the Lord* [not for fame or fortune] and doing it brings you *so much joy* you lose track of time. In Jesuit verbiage it's something that you do exclusively *for the greater glory of God.* One surgeon I know found his charism in building houses for Habitat for Humanity, as does our former President of the United States: Jimmy Carter. Another friend uses both her God given *talent* and her *charism* in choir and writing songs about her love of the Lord.

The day I realized my charism of catechesis was as my health was deteriorating, my pain was chronic and my stamina low. I still went to the weekly evening Catechism class and *God honored my sacrifice.* One night as I was arriving back home I realized that from the moment I prayed the Come Holy Spirit (always before I enter the classroom that I may remember that I am not in charge), until I reached my front door—I had no pain. We often ran overtime because the kids were so engaged that we didn't have a single "clock watcher" among us. That's a charism. I've since discovered that talents and sometimes even skills can morph into a charism. My O.C.D. is now under enough control I can call it "*enhanced* organization." When our parish decided to open a library, my talent for reading, writing and organization netted an offer to organize, set up and be librarian for the new library. I'd spend ten hours a day there, every day, if I could handle it physically. The time just flies and I adore being able to recommend books that help enrich the spiritual lives of my brothers and sisters in Christ. A charism is a perfect fit. You will also discover the *Joy in the Journey*, trying out different things to find the ways your charisms can serve your parish or community—like the little drummer boy's song—to show your unique and special love for the Lord.

Only one life, 'twil soon be past; only what's done for Christ will last.

Characteristic #6, clause #2: "...*men and women for others*"

Another challenge for me occasionally are people—plain and simple. Some days when I don't feel up to "peopling"…I use it as a verb. I post on social media a picture of a cute animal hiding under a blanket with the caption: "I can't People today!" Of course, there are times we have to muster our courage, take a deep breath, issue a couple extra prayers and go "people." But it's important to know our limits. Often, if I force myself to "people" when I ought not, I end up sinning in some snappish remark or regretful blurt. Be patient, God isn't done with me yet.

A Prayer for Hard Days

Father, hear my prayer. Grant me gospel hope in the midst of this hard day.

Help me to cling to your grace, your wisdom, and your strength.

Help me to see that you are in this and that you are with me.

In Jesus' name, Amen

I have some trouble countenancing chronic complainers and nit-pickers. Some days it takes all I can do to not talk back to grousing neighbor ladies and instead, count to ten and *imagine how Jesus would love that grumpiness away*. I ran across a prayer by Fr. James Martin S.J., and his *new version* of the Serenity prayer with his customary wit, humor and piercing insight.

New Serenity Prayer
God, grant me the serenity
To accept the people I cannot change,
Which is pretty much everyone,
Since I'm clearly not you God,
At least not the last time I checked.

And while you're at it, God,
Please give me the courage
To change what I need to change about myself,
Which is frankly a lot, since, once again,
I'm not You, which means I'm not perfect.
It's better for me to focus on changing myself
Than to worry about changing other people
Who, as you'll no doubt remember me saying,
I can't change anyway.

Finally, give me the wisdom to just shut up
Whenever I think I'm clearly smarter
Than everyone in the room,
That no one knows what they're talking about except me,
Or that I alone have all the answers.

Basically, God
Grant me the wisdom
To remember that I'm not You.   Amen.   James Martin S.J.

Clause #3, "...*whole persons of solidarity*,"

This seems like an awfully big assignment, what group can we join and help? There are a billion or so Catholics, isn't that solidarity enough? When I first saw this I imagined everyone wearing buttons like for a solidarity "campaign"…Some of mine would be would be Catholic, P.T.S.D., OCD, Broken, as well as "I heart cats" and "Yes to tofu" and maybe even one that said "don't want to *people* today." It gave me a momentary chuckle but it also made me think about what *solidarity* means religiously—and as a Spiritual Warrior.

We have *solidarity* with persecuted Christians in the Middle East; we have solidarity with refugees, we have solidarity with those who suffer, etc. But as Spiritual Warriors *we also have solidarity with the army of angels and Saints in heaven.*

"This I can Do!"

One of my first volunteer jobs at the Cathedral of St. Andrew parish, involved starting a card ministry for the homebound. I got it all set up, recruited card senders, donations of cards, stamps and envelopes and we were going great guns from the very beginning. Within the first month, I got a call from a woman who had been active in the parish for two decades but had had a medical event that affected her brain, and after surgery could no longer drive. She missed volunteering more than anything else she had been forced to give up because of her new limitations. Her husband had assumed her shopping and errand chores on top of some household duties in addition to his demanding full-time job. She was getting a bad case of restlessness and cabin fever but didn't want to burden her husband with one more thing to do for her.

She was so excited when she called me: "*This*, I can do!" she exclaimed. I can send cards, I can phone for information from relatives and I can keep the records on the computer. Please let me do this! She said she'd been praying *for God to show her how she could serve Him, in spite of her limitations!*

Within three months, she had the Card Ministry running like clockwork, had recruited other homebound parishioners to make "check in calls" or "meds reminders;" But of course, if you praised her wonderful outreach ministry, she would shake head, "No, no, what a blessing this is *for me!*" Like it says in Characteristic #6, she was *empowered to become a leader in service* [simply by the desire of her heart]. She inspired all she recruited to *become men and women for others.* She led by example and invited others to join her.

It's all about seeing a need and filling it.

I don't have the stamina to stand the long hours in soup kitchens like I used to. But I can invite the person who has no family to join my holiday dinner. One neighbor walks another's dog, three times a day, in Michigan winters, so the woman keep her beloved pet and doesn't risk falling. One lady pet sits for free so a neighbor can go out of town overnight to visit her children.

I still have the luxury of a car. Twice a month I'm available to take others to the round of grocery stores, pick up things for them or, in an emergency drive them across town at three a.m. to the all-night pharmacy so they don't have to wait until morning to start feeling better. You don't have to save the world—there are people all around you who need what *only you* could do for them. Just think how God multiplied the blessings from my simple act of sending that one woman a card! God is awesome and loves to be partners with us in caring for others.

What moves you the most with compassion? Abandoned people? Sick children? The environment? Prison Ministry? Street Evangelization? Poverty? Hunger? Remember, your talents are gifts from God. Think about how you could help accomplish the final clause of Characteristic #6: *build a more just and humane world.* God will take whatever you give and multiply it tenfold.

Are you trapped at home like I am? I belong to two Parish prayer chains that send me prayer requests via their websites—with people to pray for—first thing every morning. That's what I do. If you think that doesn't matter, you are mistaken. There is tremendous power in prayer. I would love to be able to give money to all my favorite charities—one of which is global clean and accessible water. I discovered that I can take surveys on line and for each one, I "earn" 50¢ for my selected charity. Last weekend rather than playing a favorite game on my computer, I "earned" six dollars for clean water. As my mom used to say, ad infinitum: "Where there's a will, there's a way."

Yes, I know, you know, that we don't pray to change God's mind, to bargain with God or that our prayers will change the outcome…but when we pray for the will of God, we change *ourselves.* And remember when some evil has befallen someone…this evil is *not* the will of God so we can pray for St. Michael the Archangel to do battle on that person's behalf, we can join the angels and saints in prayers for that person's recovery, or for their acceptance and peace in say, the face of a terminal diagnosis. There are so many things that we can pray for, so many things that make a difference.

I know that I have come this far, healed this much, partly because of the storm of prayers from friends and strangers who called down help for me from the heavens. I have no doubt. *Do not ever* think your prayers fall on deaf ears—especially when you are praying for someone else.

You have become a Spiritual Warrior and you are equipped to do battle for those who cannot yet don their armor, who don't know what you know. Pray for them. Show them. Lead them.

You are now empowered to become leaders in service, men and women for others,

Whole persons of solidarity, building a more just and humane world.

And God is with you every step of the way…

Chapter Ten

St. Iggy's Girl Finds the Joy!

This close to the end of the book, I'm certain some of you are asking: "Where's the *Joy* you promised?" I'm not joyful.

Are you sure?

Let's talk about Joy. Remember "rejoice always" from our foundational Scripture in I Thessalonians 5:16-18? Joy is the NOUN that causes us to VERB *rejoice.*

> Merriam-Webster defines **joy** as: *an emotion evoked by well-being, success, or good fortune or by the prospect of possessing what one desires.*

So let's do a bit of a check up and see if any joy has crept into your life while you weren't looking. That's what joy does; as we reduce our negative emotions like fear, rage, and hatred, we create a space for joy to enter and take up residence. Gradually, oh so gradually, you will notice joy has taken hold with the *prospect of possessing* more. Turning our Campaign of Healthy Habits into automatic parts of our daily lives is the best way to become aware of new joys entering your life. *Well-being, success and good fortune* are words you would have never used in the same sentence right after your life-altering trauma, but let's see if we can find some.

Remember the daily prayers *before your feet hit the floor?* For me it began with a prayer of gratitude for two, then three, then four, hours of sleep uninterrupted by nightmares—and before long, it became, and still is, a daily prayer of gratitude for a full night's sleep—or a prayer for endurance during the day if the night wasn't so peaceful. But there is JOY in my *success* of being so much better than I was, of having *made my way* toward a healthier me, even if I have not yet arrived. And when it was a good night's sleep I awake with the sense of *well-being*—another indication of joy. When that happens and I add the Armor of God, my feet hit the floor with "Okay Lord, let's take on today—together!" There's good energy in that.

The next thing I noticed was that my "startle reflex" was gradually lessening. I still have a highly-sensitive one, but I can say that I no longer lash out physically, and that being startled-to-tears by someone appearing next to me without my having heard them approach, only happens a couple times a year as opposed to several times a week. I have the *success* of easier navigation in the outside world. Which means I have *success* in being free from "terrified recluse" status.

After reconciling my mother's mental issues with my forgiveness glands, I was able to not only completely forgive her, but now, tell genuinely appreciative stories about her good points and strengths. Mother's Day is still horribly painful for me as a daughter and as a mother, but like the definition says: Joy is evoked by *the prospect* of possessing what one desires. For me, that's a list that includes reconciliation with my daughter, finding more ways to let in more joy, and to grow even closer to my Lord and Savior. So I have hope and where there is hope, there is joy. I celebrate seven years since last needing to see a therapist—because I have healthy habits to keep the healing coming. Having replaced my bad messages with God's message of Love for me, I have a sense of both, being loved and *well-being.* That's joy!

Take a moment and think deeply about what things have improved for you.
Then, take another moment and thank God for all that progress.

Speaking of spiritual health, what joy can I find to indicate progress? After nearly a decade of practicing Ignatian Spirituality and it's foundation of *praying without ceasing* (throughout-daily prayer and daily *lectio divina* immersion into God's Word) I am able to discern the high and low spirits and so I know that I am not clinically depressed but that it is the normal movement of my spirit— being strengthened by God. After frequently receiving the great blessings of the Sacraments, and working hard to cooperate with the Holy Spirit, with my spiritually-grounded therapist and my priest/spiritual directors, I can see, *real progress in my life.* I can count, much to the delight of my O.C.D., the many things have changed since I first started this journey—I am stronger, and yes, there *is* joy! I feel the joy, *well-being,* of knowing deep-in-my-heart that God loves us, more than we can ever imagine—and just the way we are, hot mess, work-in-progress, and all.

I have come to cherish and even take for granted, that Jesus walks with me, and with you, *every single step of the way.* I have learned how to forgive, and equally important, to accept God's forgiveness. I have the hope of heaven—the JOY that is the *prospect of possessing what one desires*—heavenly citizenship.

Well, you say, that's all well and good but what about the fact that I will never *physically* be the same. I lost a leg, or arm, or both. I am now in a wheelchair. I can't do what I used to do, I am "less" than whole and will never be—where's the JOY in that? This question is especially common if you must endure chronic pain or other real-life complications and obstacles.

In 1997, a film came out about an obsessive compulsive writer (Jack Nicholson) and a line of dialogue instantly resonated with *the entire nation.* Nicholson, frantically trying to see his own therapist without an appointment asks a waiting room full of patients: "What if *this is* as good as it gets?" While the movie didn't get much attention, the question was adopted into modern language almost immediately. I was baffled, it didn't seem to me to be a particularly profound question until, eight year later when I trod the long and frustrating road of my own recovery. I watched the film a second time and while, as a movie, it lagged and desperately needed editing, it did, indeed, echo my *deepest fear* back then. I'd look into my tear-swollen eyes or right after I had a public meltdown in class and was trying to catch my breath in the hallway and I'd shudder to think that *this* was as good as it was going to get.

Joy…Even in the Midst of Suffering

Turns out that this is a common and prominent question for everyone who has suffered a life-altering trauma. Am I always going to feel this way, be in this much physical, mental and/or spiritual pain? Maybe. But the really *important* answer is: never.

Ah, how God loves a paradox. In one aspect, *this* might be as good as it gets if we are talking about physical issues that cannot be overcome with medicine, science, or technology in our lifetime. It might be, if we are left with (so far) untreatable chronic pain or disease. We might not ever see again, hear again, speak again or walk again. So, yes, this might be as good as it gets *physically*—in this lifetime. But we have eternity. We also have better tools for dealing with the "unchangeable." We have, by now, a team of people (and Saints) helping us carry our cross.

Remember, God has taken on the assignment we gave Him at the beginning of our journey: and He has promised to *never quit* until His work in us reaches completion. There is JOY—a *sense of well-being* to know that God isn't finished with us yet. That we have surprises in store and that with his ability to write straight with crooked lines means we have many good things to look forward to…we have *prospects of possessing that which we desire.*

God never stops fixing us.

Having had such a challenging childhood with such contempt aimed at everything childlike, it's no wonder I never say I had a happy childhood—or a childhood. Period. And while I loved my own children even though I never understood childish behavior; I used to refer to any person's child with the same recoil I had engendered in my own mother. To me, they were OPK's: *Other People's Kids* and to be avoided at all costs. Remember what I said about God never giving up on us—on making sure we get what we *need* although we might not particularly like it?

During my "homeless period" I was taken in by my goddaughter's family—who are amazing, world-class clowns—no, literally! They are professional clowns. They also paint faces at professional sports events. While living there, I was having sporadic health issues, was attending the Seminary and substitute teaching all the while trying to find enough physical health/strength to carve a new career to support myself. Reluctantly, and I mean *reluctantly* because the idea of a swarm of OPK's set my teeth on edge I let them teach me to face paint. I was desperate to make enough money to get my own apartment. I joined them painting both children and adults for the Detroit Tigers, the Detroit Lions and the Detroit Red Wings, when my health permitted. Yes, God *surrounded me* with excited, bobbing, giggling OPK's and the occasional challenging Parent of OPK! In the beginning, I came home more mentally drained than mere physical stamina issues—PEOPLING exhausted me. But as the months passed, I not only looked forward to the events but to the children. No one was more surprised than I was. At my age, I was learning to love children—to love being around children. It was a *joy* that crept up on me. As my health deteriorated, I realized on what would be my last day face painting for the Detroit Lions, that I was overwhelmed with sadness and a sense of loss. God had given me a belated childhood. Through this, God *healed* my childhood. God *never* stops fixing us. Watch, you'll see.

It is certainly our *good fortune* to have a God who never gives up on us.

Another of my favorite books is "Redemptive Suffering" by William J. O'Malley S.J. and his subtitle says it all: "understanding suffering, living with it, growing through it." That's what many of us, my self-included, will be enduring the rest of our lives.

The first thing that struck me about his book was his candidness with his own struggles and throughout the book I have many lines highlighted.

Here are my top three favorite Fr. O'Malley's "*Pithies*" (Pithy: concise and forcefully expressive)

1. In order to really *live* you have to be hyperaware, hyper-curious and hyper humble before *What-Is* rather than *What-Ought-to Be*.

2. Wisdom is making peace with the unchangeable.

3. Only temporary greatness lies in the body; permanent greatness is lodged in the soul.

It is a small book, with great wisdom and gentle guidance. My copy is full of highlighting and tabs to special sections and I've read it a dozen times. True wisdom is never out-of-date.

I urge you to continue your book search beyond my recommendations, including the ones listed in the additional resources section at the end of the book. Favorite books are like friends you can call upon in time of need, in loneliness.

You may think since I wrote this book and talk so much about thriving and the abundant joy in my life that I am all, or mostly, physically healed. Perhaps, you might think, that I am more healed than you are, or ever will be. Remember we never compare our Cross with someone else's. It serves no useful purpose. I will tell you that I deal with many physical limitations and daily chronic pain, I still have residual effects of P.T.S.D, and medical issues that leave me, *again,* sequestered, from interaction with others and at risk.

But I do have abundant *joy, even in the midst of daily suffering.* I have the *joy* from all the things I learned, and accomplished during my spiritual journey and the ongoing journey that centers my life and hopefully my movement closer to my Lord. I have better habits for dealing with some of life's challenges and I have hope. I am free from the heaviness of anger, rage and resentment. I also have the *joy of sharing* this hope with others as an author and as parish librarian where I can guide them to books that will bring spiritual enrichment and comfort.

One of my current favorite prayers follows:

Let me not pray to be sheltered from dangers but to be fearless in facing them.
Let me not beg for the stilling of my pain, but for the courage to conquer it.
Let me not crave in anxious fear to be saved but hope for the patience to win my freedom.
Grant me that I may not be a coward, feeling Your mercy in my success alone;
But let me find the grasp of Your hand in my failure.
Rabindranath Tagore, Fruit-Gathering

And a quote by Rabindranath Tagore [a Bengali polymath—person with wide learning]

I slept and dreamt that life was joy.
I awoke and saw that life was service.
I acted and behold, service was joy.

Sounds a great deal like our 6th Characteristic doesn't it? Just as Ignatius emphasized deeds over words, we do what we can, and leave the rest to our merciful and faithful Father who will keep His promise to help us continue to move closer to spending eternity with Him. It is with that confidence, I will continue my prayers for your ongoing healing and ask for your prayers in return—and I'll see you on the other side where we will *rejoice for eternity.*
Your Sister in Christ, Thora

With space for just a couple more favorite prayers:

ACT OF HOPE:

O my God, I put my hope in you, because I am sure of your promises. Deliver me, Lord, from every evil and grant me peace in my day as I wait in joyful hope for the coming of my Savior, Jesus Christ

Healing of the Spirit and a Special Intention

Gentle Jesus, with faith in Your healing powers and confidence in Your constant compassion, I ask you to heal my suffering spirit. May my soul find rest in Your comforting love and relief from sorrow and anguish. Relying on Your love, I especially ask Your help in (name your concern.) I place my trust in Your power to heal my spirit from feelings of hopelessness, unrest and despair. Amen.

Additional Resources

Listed first topically, and then alphabetically by author

These are many of the best books I used for research or have in my cherished collection. I used many more good books but they could not all be listed here due to space or were cast aside as unacceptable—like the one that said don't forget or forgive—ever, that that was the way to strength. [I thought about inserting a horrified emoji here].

Catholicism
NRSV Catholic Bible
Ignatius Catholic Study Bible: Thessalonians, Timothy & Titus
Catechism of the Catholic Church

Discernment
General Vocational Discernment
Mahan, Brian J., "Forgetting Ourselves on Purpose,
Vocation and the ethics of ambition"

Ignatian Discernment
Gallagher, Timothy M. O.M.V. "The Discernment of Spirits,
An Ignatian Guide for Everyday Living "

Sparough, Michael J. S.J., Jim Manney and Tim Hipskind S.J.,
"What's Your Decision?" *An Ignatian approach to Decision Making*

Thibodeaux, Mark E. S.J., "God's Voice Within," *The Ignatian way to discover God's Will*

Forgiveness
Camille, Alice & Paul Bordreau "The Forgiveness Book

General
Bete, Tim, "The Raw Stillness of Heaven" (Poems that read like prayers)

Esper, Fr. Joseph "Saintly Solutions" *to Life's Common Problems*
And Vol. 2 "More Saintly Solutions"
Nouwen, Henri J.M. "With Open Hands" B*ring prayer into Your Life*

O'Malley, William J. S.J. "Yielding" *Prayers for those in need of Hope*

Healing

    Nouwen, Henri M. "The Wounded Healer" *in our own woundedness,*
        We can become a source of life for others.

    Wasco, Jan and Molly Keating, "Unlocking our Fenced in Hearts"
        by listening to the Voice of Love

Ignatian Spirituality—General

    Martin, James S.J. Ed, Becoming Who you Are" *Insights on the true self from*
        Thomas Merton and other saints
        "Between Heaven and Mirth" *Why Joy, Humor and Laughter*
        are at the Heart of the Spiritual Life"
        "Jesus a Pilgrimage" (Jesus' ministry, Gospels and Pilgrimage)
        "The Jesuit Guide to Almost Everything" *A Spirituality for*
        Real Life

    O'Malley, William J. S.J., "Redemptive Suffering" *understanding suffering,*
        living with it, growing through it
        "The Fifth Week" Second edition, [Living Ignatian Spirituality]
    Thibodeaux, Mark E. S.J. "Reimagining the Ignatian Examen" *Fresh ways to*
        Pray from your Day

WEBLINK: ignatianspirituality.com

Publishers, Ignatian: Loyola Press and Ignatius

Psychology

    Naparstek, Belleruth "Invisible Heroes" *Survivors of Trauma and How they Heal*

    Peck, M. Scott, "People of the Lie"

About the Author

The author considers herself just an ordinary person who has had the extraordinary good fortune to have had, and to continuously experience, an encounter with the Divine—every day, all around her, and in the people she meets. She holds degrees in Police Science from Northwestern Michigan College; a B.A. in English with a Creative Writing minor, a Master in Management-Servant Leadership and Theological Studies Certificate from Aquinas College in Grand Rapids, MI. She studied for a M.A. Theology at Sacred Heart Major Seminary in Detroit, MI before becoming too disabled to finish her last few classes. She has been recognized for her essays, poetry and short stories. She lives in East Lansing, Michigan with her fat cat Ms. YumYum to be near her children and grandchildren. She serves as parish librarian for Church of the Resurrection, Lansing, MI where she loves to introduce people to the rich legacy of Catholic Arts and Letters.